The Church and the
Jewish People

The Church and the Jewish People

A Commentary on the Second Vatican Council's Declaration on the Relation of the Church to Non-Christian Religions

Augustin Cardinal Bea, S.J.

Translated by
Philip Loretz, S.J.

HARPER & ROW, PUBLISHERS

New York

LIBRARY OF CONGRESS CATALOG CARD NUMBER 66–20790

Contents

Introduction

The relation of the Church with the Jewish people is a two thousand year old problem, as old as Christianity itself. It became much more acute, particularly in view of the ruthless policy of extermination inflicted upon millions of Jews by the Nazi regime in Germany. And so it has attracted the attention of the Second Vatican Council. After a protracted period of preparation and many arduous discussions, the Declaration "On the attitude of the Church towards non-Christian religions" has taken shape and has been widely acclaimed as a milestone in the history of the relations between the Church and the Jewish people. That it does deserve such a description emerges from the single fact that it marks the first occasion when an Ecumenical Council has considered the problem in so explicit a manner. Furthermore, instead of confining itself to a purely practical decree or a simple condemnation of anti-semitism, the Council has approached the problem in the wider context of the relations of the Church with non-Christian religions in general. At the same time it has sought a solution of it at a profoundly biblical level. This is done in such a way that the Declaration may well be said to offer valuable directives for all Christians, irrespective of denominational diversities.

The importance of the document has been increased by the publicity given by the world press to the long preparations and lively discussions devoted to it, as well as to the outcome of the final ballot. From the point of view of the Catholic Church itself, the moral weight of the document has been very considerably enhanced by the fact that it was finally approved by a majority of over ninety-six per cent, so that its adoption was virtually unanimous.

The sole purpose of this book is to offer a succinct explanation of the document. Various statements released to the press after the promulgation of the Declaration, especially those emanating from Jewish sources, while recognising the great value of the document also emphasised that its beneficial effects would very largely depend upon the degree to which it was fully understood, assimilated and put into practice. This proviso obviously applies to all the documents issued by the Council, but it is especially relevant in the present instance because of the long centuries of strained relationships, antipathies and difficulties affecting both Jews and Christians alike. The aim of this commentary, therefore, is to assist in this process of assimilation and to help towards producing a greater awareness of the problem as a whole. At the same time we shall try to explain the scriptural foundations of the document and to discuss its concrete suggestions and the ways and means of putting them into practice. This commentary is not intended for specialists but is addressed to people of ordinary education, since it is precisely upon them that the practical implementation of the Declaration will depend.

It will be clear that this commentary does not purport to offer a complete study of the whole vast and complicated problem of Judaism and anti-semitism. As I have already had occasion to remark in the Council chamber itself, the painful phenomenon of anti-semitism draws its sustenance neither principally nor exclusively from religious sources. Many other factors, political, national, psychological, social and economic, enter into it. None of these will be discussed here. Although it is obvious they have their own weight and importance, the Church considers that the best contribution she can make to a gradual solution of the two thousand year old problem lies in her spiritual and religious sources and in the attitude of the faithful. She wants them to see the religious aspects of the problem and apply to it in all honesty the teaching of divine revelation, above all that of the New Testament.

In the light of what has been said above, the exact meaning of the title of this book will be apparent. In substance it is taken from the Council's document itself. This, in the section dealing with the Jews, more or less defines its terms of reference as follows: "As the Council searches into the mystery of the Church, it remembers the bond which spiritually ties the people of the New Covenant to the offspring of Abraham." So it deals with the relationship, past and present, between the Church and the Jewish people. It is concerned with showing what was the nature of this relationship during the period of preparation for Christianity in Old Testament times and during its realisation, and what its nature should always be in the daily life of the Church and of its members. And it is the Church herself who is speaking through the medium of a document of the Council, in which she is evidently teaching in a solemn and univers- ally binding way. The present study has no other purpose than to high-light the Church's teaching and reveal it in all its splendour.

To define the scope of our study a little more precisely, it will be as well to emphasise the meaning which we attach to the term "Jewish people". In view of what we have just said about the title of the book it will be clear that we interpret the expression in the same sense as the Declaration, that is to say, in the sense in which it is used in holy scripture itself. The term indicates, therefore, those descendants of Abraham whom God chose for himself and constituted as the people of Israel, with whom he concluded an alliance, slowly educating them and revealing himself and his salvific designs to them in the course of their history—and all this in preparation for the coming of Christ and the redemption of mankind. From this, the purely and exclusively religious character of the Declaration and the present commentary becomes abundantly clear. It is noteworthy that during the preparation of the Declaration the greatest possible care was taken to emphasise its religious character in such a way as to exclude the possibility of any sort of political interpretation, or at least to make the falsity of any such construction apparent.[1]

---

[1] In passing, we may take note of a *terminological* question. A writer has recently made the following distinctions: "From the *ethnological* aspect the Jewish people, or better still the Jewish race, comprise all those individuals who are descendants of the twelve tribes of Israel, no matter what their religion or their nationality may be. From the *political* standpoint, however, the Jewish 'people' cannot mean only those Jews who are citizens of the Republic of Israel since this would exclude large numbers of the Jews of the diaspora who have not chosen to return to Palestine." The author concludes that the Council has no reason to concern itself with the Jews from an ethnological or a political point of view but solely from a religious standpoint. As a consequence he speaks only of the "*Jewish religion*", or if one prefers, of "*Judaism*", this term being taken to indicate the community of those who, irrespective of time or place, profess the mosaic religion and therefore regard themselves as "God's chosen people".

Apart from any other remarks which might have to be made on the question of terminology, the crucial point lies for us in the fact that holy scripture still speaks of the people of Israel in St Paul's time (cf. Romans 9–11, esp. 11:1f.) when there was a very wide dispersal of the Jews all over the Roman Empire and when, in

In connection with the specifically religious character of the Declaration and of this study, mention must be made of the *method* of procedure adopted in the present commentary. Its purpose is to explain a conciliar document which is a manifestation of the most solemn teaching of the Church's magisterium. Now the function of the magisterium is essentially that of making known the guaranteed religious teaching of Christ as it is written down in the Old and New Testaments and is gradually and ever more fully unfolded by the Church over the centuries. For this reason, the present commentary will try to explain the Council's Declaration above all in the light of holy scripture, appealing to the latter not as purely historical documents but as religious writings, scripture inspired by God and therefore the word of God. At the same time we shall endeavour, as far as possible, to examine in particular the data of the Old Testament, in order to give real support to encounter between Christians and Jews, since the writings of the Old Testament form the main meeting place for both of them.

Obviously, in the course of explaining the Declaration, we shall have to give some consideration to the criticisms which have been levelled here and there against the document. We do not, however, intend to defend the Declaration, the work of the Council or that of the Secretariat for

addition, the new people of God, "Israel according to the Spirit", the Church, had been constituted. As has been seen above, the same language was also used in the text of the Constitution on the Church. It is true that the Declaration on the Relation of the Church to Non-Christian Religions does not employ the term "Jewish people" (although it did occur in the earlier redactions). The reason for this, however, is not that this expression is illegitimate in itself but that it might give rise to misunderstanding from a political point of view or to false theological interpretations, as though the Jewish people were still the people of God in the sense of an institution for the salvation of mankind. (More will be said later on this point. See ch. 7.)

Christian unity which had the task of preparing it. In fact
we do not think in any way that this document is absolutely
perfect—something in any case humanly impossible—and
that therefore it must be defended at all costs as a whole
and in every detail. Not at all. My only desire is to enable
the reader to understand the meaning of its more difficult
points and the reasons why this or that formulation was
given to them. It is hardly surprising that there should
be difficulties enough in a document which deals with a
problem two thousand years old in scarcely five hundred
words; hence the need for some clarification in order
that the Declaration may produce the greatest possible
fruit.

If we take into account the enormous strides which the
Church has made into a relatively new field, we shall not
be surprised that besides the difficulties inherent in the
problem itself and in the way in which it is handled in the
Declaration, still others should arise when many different
types of readers, whether members of the Church itself or
non-Christians, scrutinise the document and attempt to
arrive at an exact interpretation of it.[1] We do not propose

---

[1] We have used the expression "*relatively new*" to indicate that it is not the first
occasion in recent times that the Church has stated her position on the relations of
Christians with the Jewish people, especially on the question of anti-semitism.
We are thinking of the well-known declaration of the Congregation of the Holy
Office of 25 March 1928, which stated: ". . . In its charity the Apostolic See
often protected the Jewish people against unjust molestation. And hence it
condemns all forms of hostile rivalry between peoples and consequently it very
specially condemns hatred against a people, chosen of old by God, that hatred
which today is commonly called anti-semitism. . . ." (cf. A.A.S., 20, 1928, p. 104).
    Note also the famous declaration of Pius XI, who said, " 'Look on these offerings
with favour and contentment . . .' We read this prayer at the most solemn
moment of the Mass, after the consecration, when the divine victim is really
offered. 'The sacrifice of Abel, the sacrifice of Abraham, the sacrifice of Melchizedek.' In three strokes, three lines, three steps, the whole religious history of

at this point to enter into a discussion of the difficulties presented by the various concepts used in the Declaration, as for example "election" or "chosen people", though we shall have occasion to do so in the course of this book. We would like, however, to mention briefly some difficulties which are not examined in the Declaration and which will likewise be disregarded in our commentary.

For Catholics, one of the chief difficulties will be the task of correctly integrating the teaching of the Declaration with what they have already been more or less explicitly taught. For them, both the general principles of the Declaration and their application as presented therein will be somewhat new. We believe, notwithstanding, that taken as a whole the present study will serve to embrace all that and to demonstrate the biblical foundation of this teaching.

Yet another difficulty arises. Anyone with some knowledge of Church history and particularly of ancient Christian writers and of the Fathers of the Church will ask how we can explain the attitude adopted by *some* of the Fathers on the present question. We are thinking, for example, of some of the statements of St Ambrose or St John Chrysostom,

mankind. The sacrifice of Abel, at the time of Adam. The sacrifice of Abraham: the era of the religion and the marvellous history of Israel. The sacrifice of Melchizedek: the adumbration of the Christian religion and times. A magnificent text! Every time we read it we cannot help being deeply moved: 'Sacrificium Patriarchae nostri Abrahame.' Note that Abraham is called our father, our ancestor. Anti-semitism is incompatible with the ideas and the sublime reality expressed in this passage. Anti-semitism is a revolting movement in which we Christians can have no part. It is impossible for Christians to participate in anti-semitism. We acknowledge the right of every man to defend himself, to use suitable means to defend himself against everything which threatens his legitimate interests. But anti-semitism is inadmissible. Spiritually we are semites." (An allocution to the pilgrimage of Radio Catholique Belge, 6 September 1938, from *La libre Belgique* of 14 September 1938, reported in *La Documentation Catholique*, vol. XXXIX, 1938, col. 1460.)

which are either seemingly or actually in contradiction
to the principles contained in the Declaration. Since we
cannot deal properly with this problem here, we must
rest content with recalling the principle on which such
phenomena should be judged. Discrepancies of this sort are
not confined exclusively to the present question but are to
a certain extent encountered in all branches of the Church's
doctrine and in the practice of the Christian life. First of all,
it must be remembered that often when the Fathers make
unfavourable or hostile remarks concerning the Jews, they
do not refer specifically to members of the Jewish people
as such but rather to a particular attitude of mind, namely
the refusal of belief in the Gospels and sometimes an unjust,
if not positively violent, opposition to Christianity which as
a matter of historical fact often accompanied such a refusal.
This manner of speaking on the part of the Fathers corres-
ponds to that used in the New Testament itself, for example
by St Paul and above all in the Gospel of St John, to which
we shall refer again in the course of this commentary.
However, to give a concrete example here and now, St
Paul wrote to the Thessalonians about the Jews as follows:
"They killed both the Lord Jesus and the prophets, and
drove us out and displease God and oppose all men . . . so
as always to fill up the measure of their sins. But God's
wrath has come upon them at last" (1 Thessalonians 2:15 ff.).
Is this perhaps anti-semitism? No; it is simply indignation
at the unjust persecution of Christians at Thessalonica
which reminded St Paul, in his turn, of all he himself had
suffered in so many cities and still more of the sufferings
inflicted upon Jesus himself. This reaction to the injustice
perpetrated by certain sections of the Jews does not, however,

prevent the same apostle from writing, with ardent love, that he could wish that he himself were cut off from Christ "for the sake of his brethren, his kinsmen by race" (cf. Romans 9:3). Certainly, therefore, it would be a mistake to use these words from the Epistle to the Thessalonians in order to justify a doctrine of anti-semitism and to blame the Jews as such for every sort of ill. It is necessary to interpret this passage in its concrete historical context and on the basis of the actual circumstances to which it refers. A similar necessity arises in the case of the statements of the Fathers which we have mentioned above. Each case must be examined on its own merits to see what precise meaning should be attributed to this or that unfavourable comment on the Jews and to ascertain what concrete facts prompted it. It is nothing more than an elementary requirement of truth and justice that each text should be interpreted in the framework of its historical context.

Naturally, we do not pretend that such a concrete, historical interpretation will explain away every action or statement on the part of authoritative persons in the history of the Church which is contrary to the spirit and the letter of the new conciliar document. The Church finds no difficulty—in proven cases—in acknowledging that one of its members, or some particular or local church, has erred. A somewhat sensational incident of this kind has recently occurred in the suppression of the cult paid for centuries to Blessed Little Simon of Trent. This man was honoured as a martyr who was killed by the Jews in hatred of the faith. When, however, recent critical researches revealed certain contradictions in the acts of the process which, at least, raised doubts as to the fact of his murder by the Jews, the ecclesiastical authorities did not hesitate to acknolwedge the error and to forbid the cult in question.[1]

Love of truth certainly sometimes requires that we should acknowledge our faults. Nevertheless, both love of truth and justice also demand that we should refrain from judging statements made in earlier times by the standards which the Church has only attained in the light of the progressive growth in our understanding of doctrine extending over many centuries. It is common knowledge that such a progress and development does in fact take place in the explicit interpretation of the teaching entrusted by Christ to his Church. It is a very real process which can be easily demonstrated. According to St Paul's familiar doctrine, the Church is a living organism which grows and develops until "we all attain to the unity of the faith and of the knowledge of the Son of God, to mature manhood, to the measure of the stature of the fullness of Christ" (cf. Ephesians 4:13 ff.). The Church is made up of men, and just as it follows the laws of supernatural life imparted to it by Christ, so also it follows those of human life. How can we wonder, then, if not all its members have at all times succeeded in fully realising certain consequences and implications of its teaching, even when caught up in difficult circumstances, or have failed to put them into practice under unfavourable conditions. It would certainly be wrong to deny that there has been weakness in the Church upon occasion. It would be

---

[1] It is significant that the decree bears the date 28 October, 1965, the day of the promulgation of the Declaration. It was based on the work of W. P. Eckert, "Il beato Simonino negli 'Atti' del processo di Trento contro gli Ebrei", in *Studi Trentini di Scienze Storiche*, 44, 1915, pp. 193–221. It consists substantially of the articles which this author published in the collection *Judenhass—Schuld der Christen?* which is mentioned later in our bibliographical note.

equally unjust, however, to gauge responsibility and pass judgement on men of past centuries according to the degree of enlightenment which has only been achieved after centuries of hard thinking, of gaining experience and of making efforts to be realistic.

Another series of difficulties which the Council document is likely to encounter—and, perhaps in even greater measure, the present commentary—concerns the members of the Jewish people itself. Clearly this book is written just as much *directly* for them as for Christians. It speaks *to* Christians *about* the Jews, and is therefore of the greatest interest to the latter. It is essential that Christians should be fair in their judgements about the Jews but it is equally important that the Jews should know what they think. Otherwise the two parties cannot arrive at a mutual understanding. It is precisely here that the difficulty arises. Respect for the truth demands that certain things should be said in the course of this commentary which do no great credit to the Jews, and though it is our duty to express them fairly, moderately and charitably, they must still be said. On the other hand, it is only natural that the dislike and unfriendliness, which the Jews have had to put up with for so many centuries, and the terrible policy of extermination inflicted upon them by the Nazis should have made them peculiarly sensitive to any adverse criticism of any particular Jew or class of Jews at any period of their long history. It is scarcely to be expected, therefore, that they will be able to understand immediately all that is said in the following chapters. To meet this difficulty I would like to say a few preliminary words here about two difficulties in particular which I feel they are likely to encounter in reading this book.

The first is concerned with the *less favourable* statements which will be made about certain groups or classes of Jews at a particular historical period, namely, at the time of the life and death of Christ and of the founding of the first Christian communities. I am well aware that they do not agree with us either with regard to the authenticity or to the evaluation of the facts concerned. All the same I would ask them at least to consider the following undeniable psychological fact: Christians continually read the New Testament and are therefore concerned with the facts as reported in the books which they regard as sacred, just as the Jews do the books of the Old Testament. Given this fact, any disquisition on the proper attitude of Christians towards the Jews must necessarily take facts into account. They cannot be entirely ignored or disguised. It is only by explaining the right and proper way of looking at them and weighing them up that there can be any hope of persuading both Christans and Jews to take up a correct and mutually-helpful attitude towards them, inspired by truth, justice and charity. We cannot avoid speaking to them, but what really matters is the way in which we do so. I would therefore beg all my readers, particularly our Jewish brethren, to believe, as a provisional hypothesis at least, that whatever is said here will be said exclusively in accordance with the norms of truth, justice and love.

We shall also try to approach this task with due *humility*. Unfavourable comments will not be presented out of any sense of the superiority of Christians over the Jews, still less with any desire to discredit any individual Jew or the Jewish people as a whole. We Christians are the first, perhaps, to speak in this way of our own defects and transgressions.

St Paul wrote: "We have already shown that all men, both Jews and Gentiles, are under the power of sin, as it is written: 'None is righteous, no, not one'," and continued for several verses in the same vein (cf. Romans 3:9-18). He also wrote of himself: "The saying is sure and worthy of full acceptance, that Christ Jesus came into the world to save sinners. And I am the foremost of sinners" (1 Timothy 1:15). Again, he said to the Ephesians: "We were by nature children of wrath, like the rest of mankind" (Ephesians 2:3). St James, too, wrote: "For we all make many mistakes" (James 3:2). And if we want a more recent example, let us recall that at the beginning of the second session of the Council, Pope Paul VI solemnly asked pardon of God and of our non-Catholic Christian brethren for any faults committed by the Catholic Church which have contributed to the tragic divisions among Christians in past centuries. In the Declaration itself, in the section dealing with the Jewish people, the Church reminds the faithful that Christ voluntarily underwent his passion and death "because of the sins of all mankind".

Another difficulty which I have often encountered in contacts with Jews is the fear that our only desire is to "convert" them—a word which all too often brings back very painful memories, and that whatever the Church does is ultimately directed to this hidden purpose. And by "convert" is understood, if not use of actual force and pressure, at least the intention of seducing men by subtle argument and astute manipulation to betray their own conscience. However, on this count also the Church has nothing to hide. In the conciliar document she explicitly and openly declares that it is both her duty and her desire to preach

Christ who is "the way, the truth and the life", in whom
God has reconciled all things to himself. From the beginning
it is pointed out that the aim of the document is to investigate
all that men have *in common* and which encourages them to
live together and fulfil their common destiny; not, therefore,
to dwell upon what divides and differentiates them. The
Declaration further affirms very clearly that the Church
in no way rejects all that is true and holy in religions other
than the one she herself preaches. In addition, in the conciliar
document on religious liberty, the Church solemnly declares
as her own teaching the duty and the right of every man to
pursue truth and justice according to the dictates of his own
conscience, unimpeded and untrammelled. In the Declaration with which this commentary deals, she exhorts her own
members to recognise, preserve and promote whatever
is spiritually, morally, socially or culturally valuable in
religions different from their own. According to the intention of the Church, it is a question of mutual exchange
among men of all that each possesses, especially in the
spiritual domain, in conformity with the most absolute
love of truth, in justice and liberty, in an atmosphere of
mutual respect and goodwill. What man could reasonably
and honestly object to such an exchange? Do we not
today proclaim the right of man to the benefit of reliable
information and instruction, the right to the truth, and are
we not prepared to fight for them? Is religious truth, which
concerns man's deepest desires and highest destiny, perhaps
of less importance and less worthy to be promoted and
brought within the grasp of any man to become his entirely
free possession? Furthermore, in our case we are not concerned with a merely human good which can be discovered

and acquired by human efforts alone and which is conferred by one man on another with a certain sense of superiority, as something which the giver has got as a result of his own natural talent and efforts. No, we are concerned with benefits which are purely and simply the gratuitous gift of God to mankind. Whoever transmits them does nothing more than pass on what he himself has received through no merit of his own. There is, therefore, no humiliation for the receiver and no kudos for the transmitting medium. What cause, then, is there for fear or mistrust?

So much, then, must suffice to make the aim of this commentary crystal clear and to establish mutual trust between author and reader. Life today teaches us ever more insistently how important is confidence of this kind in every department of human activity, especially when men of different mentalities come together in love of truth, in justice and in charity to serve freely the welfare and tranquility of the large human family.

I

A short note on the
history of the document

Before the first reading of the Declaration was put to the
vote in November, 1964, in the course of a few introductory
remarks, I compared its growth with that of the mustard seed
in the Gospel parable, a comparison which is applicable in
several respects. Pope John XXIII received me in audience
on 18 September, 1960 and charged the Secretariat for
Christian Unity with the task of preparing a Declaration
dealing with the Jewish people. In so doing, he took a
second and more decisive step along the road which he
had opened up on Good Friday, 1959. It was on that day,
during the solemn liturgy, that he had read out the order to
omit the adjective "perfidious" from the customary prayer
for the Jews. Although, to modern ears, this adjective has a
pejorative ring, in the medieval latin of the time of the
prayer's composition it simply meant "unbelieving". This
gesture excited Jewish public opinion and raised high hopes.
Even Pope John, however, could not have foreseen the
proportions which the task he had allotted to the Secretariat
would later assume. The subsequent history of the Declaration was notable because of great difficulties, not all of which
were theological, for some were partly due to the unhappy

political circumstances of our time. It was these very difficulties which made it essential for the document to be a very carefully balanced statement. They also served, bit by bit, to give it the greater breadth it now has as a result of its extension to include the attitude of the Church to non-Christian religions in general and to place the Jewish problem in a wider context.

The first of these difficulties arose in June 1962 when the first schema, dealing only with the Jews and hammered out by the Secretariat in the course of many long sessions, was included in the agenda of the Central Preparatory Commission of the Council.

Unfortunately, at this precise moment, news came through that certain Jewish organisations were to be represented at Rome in connection with the Ecumenical Council and this produced some vociferous protests on the part of the Arabs. It was, therefore, considered prudent to allay anxiety by removing the schema on the Jews from the agenda of the Council.

At this stage, the President of the Secretariat again approached Pope John XXIII who sent to the Council a personal note which included the following comment: "Having carefully examined Cardinal Bea's report, we unreservedly associate ourselves with the burden and responsibility of a concern which we must make our own" (the note is dated 13 December 1962). In the following months, it was decided as a matter of prudence to present the schema in the wider context of the attitude of the Church to non-Christian religions in general and it was in this form that it was put before the fathers of the Council on 18 November 1963, as the fourth chapter of the Decree on

Ecumenism, with the title "The Attitude of Catholics to non-Christians, especially the Jews".

In deference to the truth, however, it must be confessed that in this schema there were only three introductory lines which referred to non-Christians in general while the whole of the rest dealt with the Jews. The really full and actual amplification seen in the Declaration owed its origin to the debates which took place during the second session of the Council. It was the Council fathers from the Near East, in particular, who insisted on the inclusion of a reference to Islam, while others went still further in demanding an entirely general approach to include all non-Christian religions.

In order to satisfy these demands, a schema was worked out on broader lines after the second session of the Council and was submitted to discussion at the end of September 1964. An emended text was put to the vote after its first reading on 20 November of that year. The result of this ballot was as follows.

Total votes	1,996
Yes	1,651
No	99
Yes, with reservations	242

According to the Council ruling "Yes, with reservations" is counted as basically positive, so that the text obtained nearly 95 per cent of the votes in its favour.

At this juncture there arose a more disturbing problem which had more or less dogged the whole progress of the document. The result of the ballot on the first reading gave rise to so much popular agitation in the Near East that for a time there was reason for grave anxiety, and serious thought had now to be given to ways and means of preventing similar unrest at the moment of the Council's definitive approval of the document. There is no point in discussing the causes of these misgivings and it is enough to say that they were largely due to misunderstandings arising mainly from lack of sufficient information, which left the public at the mercy of irresponsible propaganda either for or against the document. It became imperative, therefore, that the final revision of the text, and especially its submission to the vote at the last session of the Council, should be accompanied by the closest possible liasion with the representatives of both the Catholic and non-Catholic ecclesiastical authorities of the Near East and that close attention should be paid to the organs of information and every assistance given to them.

Everything possible was done to meet the objections raised by the 242 fathers. On two occasions (in March and in May 1965), between the sessions of the Council, the text was submitted to further minute examination. In addition a series of visits were made to the Near East to make contact with the principal Catholic and non-Catholic ecclesiastical authorities in order to ascertain their difficulties and their wishes in the matter. In this way the final revision of the text was arrived at and was put to the vote on 14 and 15 October 1965. In a statement which I made immediately before the ballot I pointed out that the revision of the text had been carried out with the sole purpose of rendering it clearer and more precise while *faithfully preserving the sense* of the original text which had been approved by a large majority. At the second reading the ballot was as follows:

Total votes	2,023
Yes	1,763
No	250
No vote	10

Great, then, was the general surprise when, at the final ballot on 28 October 1965, in the public Congregation, the 250 No's unexpectedly fell to 88. The actual figures were:

Total votes	2,312
Yes	2,221
No	88
With reservations (disallowed)	2
No vote	1

In comparison with the first ballot in 1964, the absolute number of No's fell slightly, whereas there was a massive increase of 328 in the votes in favour of the Declaration.

The final approval and promulgation of the Declaration produced yet another very welcome surprise. Although, as was stated above, everything possible had been done between the sessions to forestall difficulties and disquiet arising from lack of sufficient official information, there was still some reason for apprehension. In the event, apart from a few sporadic adverse reactions, the promulgation of the document was calmly received and on the whole it was correctly interpreted.

All in all, it may fairly be said that the evolution of this document offers an encouraging example of loyal and brotherly collaboration even though it was approached from widely divergent points of view. It shows, moreover, that determined efforts to promote brotherly understanding, even in the face of unavoidable difficulties and delays, despondency and uneasiness are blessed by the Lord, the God of peace, and ultimately come to fruition.[1]

[1] Since an erudite bibliography of our subject does not come within the scope of this commentary, we shall confine ourselves to mentioning a few recent works which have appeared in the climate of the Council and in connection with the discussions in the Council chamber: G. Baum, *The Jews and the Gospel*, Westminster (Maryland), 1961, (recently republished under the title *Is the New Testament Antisemitic?*); G. Caprile, *La Responsibilità degli ebrei nella crocefissione di Gesù*, 2nd ed., Florence, 1964; L. M. Carli, "La questione guidaica davanti al Concilio Vaticano II", in *Plestra del Clero*, XLIV, 1965, pp. 185–203; *Id.* "È possible discutere serenamente della questione giudaica?", *ibid.*, pp. 465–467; P. Demann, *Les Juifs. Foi et Destinée*, Paris, 1961; W. P. Eckert, E. L. Ehrlich, *Judenhass— Schuld der Christen?*, Essen, 1964; T. Federici, *Israele vivo*, (Quaderni Missionari), Turin, 1962; W. D. Marsch & K. Thieme, *Christen und Juden—Ihr Gegenüber vom Apostelkonzil bis heute*, Mainz-Göttingen, 1961; J. M. Oesterreicher, *The Israel of God*, Englewood Cliffs (N.J.), 1963; J. Toulat, *Juifs mes frères*, Paris, 1962. Nearly all these works give ample bibliographies on the subject, including the history of the problem (for the latter see especially Marsch-Thieme & Eckert-Ehrlich). For further references see Freiburger Rundbrief, published by G. Luckner, 1948 ff., Year XII; *The Bridge; Yearbook of Judaeo-Christian Studies*, 1955 ff. "Elenchus Suppletorius ad Elenchum Bibliographicum Biblicum", in *Verbum Domini*, 40, 1942, 56–61; "Elenchus Bibliographicus", in *Biblica*, 1965, vol. 4, under "Christiani et Judaei, olim et hodie".

II

The general human implications
of the Declaration

Somewhat in the customary manner of such documents, the Declaration opens with a consideration of the norms according to which its general principles will be developed and shows the spirit animating the whole document and underlying all its detailed considerations and directives. The fundamental importance of this introductory section of the Declaration is therefore evident.

It supplies an answer to the following four questions.

1. What is the exact purpose of the Declaration?
2. What forms the basis of the action towards which the Declaration is directed?
3. What, in general, is the function of religion in this field?
4. What is the Church's attitude, and what should the attitude of the faithful be, towards non-Christian religions?

The purpose of the Declaration

It is concerned with promoting the unity of the human family in every possible way. In this, says the document, the

Church is prompted by the consideration of the world of today in which "the human race is being drawn ever closer together, and the ties between different peoples are becoming stronger." Such a consideration not only reminds the Church of her general obligation to promote unity and charity among men, and therefore, among nations, but also greatly increases her sense of its urgency. In what way then can she promote it? Above all by calling attention to what men share and therefore to what encourages them to practice "sharing" and "togetherness" in the fulfilment of their common destiny.

This definition of its purpose reveals the vigour and realism of the Declaration. It warns us not to expect from it a complete picture of individual religions with a catalogue of the ways in which they resemble and differ from the Catholic faith. Rather, it is chiefly concerned with emphasising the common elements in accordance with the precise requirements of its declared purpose. Prior to the ballot on the Declaration, I made the following statement in the Council chamber itself: "In this Declaration, the Council seeks to point to the bonds which exist between men and between religions and which provide a basis for dialogue and collaboration between them. For this reason it has devoted its attention to all that draws men together and promotes communication between them. In such a task we must naturally proceed with prudence but also with mutual trust and with charity." This statement should also serve to allay the anxiety of those who fear that the Church intends to exploit the dialogue proposed as a subterfuge for staging a discussion, polemical perhaps, on interconfessional differences and thus to gain the upper hand over others by arguing in a bitter and unyielding spirit. Nothing could be further from the truth. Its purpose is simply and solely to foster unity and promote the practice of "sharing" and "togetherness" among men.

The foundations of unity

The Declaration points to the growing unification of the world as one of the motives that led to its inception but immediately adds another far stronger reason, derived from the treasure house of the Church's teaching which is contained in the divine revelation of the Old and New Testaments. The words defining this motive could well be branded in letters of fire on every international organisation:

> One is the community of all peoples, one their origin, for God made the whole human race to live on all the face of the earth. One also is their final goal, God. His providence, his manifestations of goodness, his saving design extend to all men, until that time when the elect will be united in the Holy City, the city ablaze with the glory of God, where the nations will walk in its light (Declaration, 1, Preamble).

This highly condensed passage may be compared in some ways with the well-known text in St Paul's Epistle to the Ephesians, in which, speaking of unity among Christians, the apostle sums up all the most powerful reasons for that unity (Ephesians 4:4-6).

> There is one body and one Spirit, just as you were called to the one hope that belongs to your call, one Lord, one faith, one baptism, one God and Father of us all.

Similarly, in speaking of the unity of the whole human family, our document points to our unity in God as the indestructible foundation on which it rests: all men come from God, our creator, we journey back to him as our final goal, and on this journey we are the objects of his providence and his gracious guidance. God wishes to bring all men to salvation in union with himself and he guides them to this happy final state.

In the document, man's common *origin* is expressed in the words taken from St Paul's famous speech on the Areopagus: God "who gives to all men life and breath and everything. And he made from one every nation of men to live on all the face of the earth, having determined allotted periods and the boundaries of their habitation" (Acts 17:25-6). This text, in its turn, echoes the teaching which can be said to pervade the whole of the Old Testament. A number of texts affirm in a general way that all creation takes its origin from God, man included: "For in six days the Lord made heaven and earth and the sea and all that is in them" (Exodus 20:11; cf. Psalm 144(145):6; Acts 17:24). In others, particular emphasis is placed on the fact that all men owe their origin and existence to God: "Thus says God, the Lord... who gives breath to the people upon the earth and spirit to those who walk in it" (Isaiah 42:5). The author of the Book of Wisdom invokes God as follows: "God of my fathers, and Lord of mercy, who hast made all things with thy word. And by thy wisdom hast appointed man, that he should have dominion over the creatures that were made by thee" (Wisdom 9:1-2). And once again, the idea which re-echoes the story of Genesis, namely that it is God who gave man the earth for a dwelling-place: "The heavens are the Lord's heavens, but the earth he has given to the sons of men" Psalm (114) 115:16; cf. Isaiah 45:18).

Besides their common origin, men also share a common destiny: God is every man's final goal. Speaking of man's creation, the Book of Ecclesiasticus says "God filled them with knowledge and understanding and showed them both good and evil . . . Moreover he gave them instructions and the law of life. He made an everlasting covenant with them and showed them his justice and his judgements" (Ecclesiasticus 17:6, 9ff.). Since then, man was made in the image of God, his *summum bonum* will necessarily be found in God in some way, or rather it will be God himself. For this reason the author of the Book of Wisdom, addressing God, says: "For to know thee is perfect justice; and to know thy justice and thy power is the root of immortality" (Wisdom 15:3).

It is in the New Testament, however, that man's goal, God, is made especially clear and specific. In his first Epistle, St Peter writes: "God the author of all grace, who has called you to his eternal glory in Christ" (1 Peter 5:10; cf. 1 Thessalonians 2:12). In the last hours of his life, when speaking of his mission and addressing his Father who gave him power over all men so as to give eternal life to all those entrusted to him, Jesus will say: "And now this is eternal life, that they may know thee, the only true God, and Jesus Christ whom thou hast sent" (John 17:2ff.). Here we may note especially the statement that the Son has been given power over all men in order to give them eternal life. In Christ, then, all men are called to eternal life, to the knowledge of God, to that royal banquet to which Jesus compared the kingdom of God and which is, to change the metaphor, the finishing post, the point in the race of life run by man. To every man without distinction is given the ineffable greatness of becoming like God, of becoming a son of God, as we are told by the apostle John: "Beloved, we are God's children now; it does not yet appear what we shall be, but we know that when he appears we shall be like him, for we shall see him as he is" (1 John 3:2).

It is useful to note how the *common* density of all mankind begins to be revealed in the Old Testament. Although, in fact, the revelation of the Old Testament was already destined for all mankind, it was primarily and directly given to Israel, the chosen people of the Old Covenant. All the same, even in Old Testament times, the universality of the message sent by God to mankind through the Jewish people becomes ever more clearly outlined. In fact, just as it is already clearly revealed in the Old Testament that God is the creator of the whole world and of all nations, so we meet there, little by little, the various consequences of this teaching. The well-known catalogue of the nations in the tenth chapter of Genesis reveals that all men form a single family from which no nation is excluded, a family which finds its origin in the first couple created by God.

Again, in the Old Testament we find expressed the idea of God's fatherly care for all peoples and his love for them. Even the vocation of Abraham was for the benefit of all nations: "And in thee all the nations of the earth shall be blessed" (Genesis 12:3). God's fatherly solicitude is manifested in a moving manner in the story of Nineveh and the prophet Jonah's mission and preaching. This prophet was sufficiently niggardly to be displeased when God showed mercy to the people of Nineveh who had become converted as a result of his preaching. "But it displeased Jonah exceedingly and he was angry", says the Bible. What is more, the prophet more or less reproved the Lord: "For I know that thou art a gracious God and merciful, and easy to forgive evil." And in his misery Jonah prayed to the Lord to let him die: "It is better for me to die than to live." But God proceeded to teach him a lesson through the well-known symbolic incident of the castor oil plant and later said to him: "Should I not pity Nineveh, that great city, in which there are more than a hundred and twenty thousand persons who do not know their right hand from their left, and also much cattle" (Jonah 4:11 cf. also Jeremiah 16:8).

Thus the idea that all nations are included in Israel's calling, is gradually traced out especially in the exhortations addressed to them to adore and call upon God together with Israel (cf. Psalm 46 (47):2; 65(66):8; 96(97):7; 97(98):4; 116(117):1; cf. Romans 15:10ff.).

In his well-known vision, the prophet Isaiah sees all the nations converging upon the temple of the Lord on Zion (Isaiah 2:1-4; cf. Micah 4:1-3). Similarly, he declares that in messianic times, when the Lord appears over Jerusalem, all nations will come to his light (Isaiah 60:1-9). The psalmist likewise predicts that after the passion and glorification of the suffering Messiah, "All the ends of the earth shall remember and shall turn to the Lord and all the families of the nations shall adore in his sight" (Psalm 21(22):28); this point is well illustrated by those psalms which hymn the universality of the kingdom of God at the Messiah's coming (Psalm 71(72): 10ff.; 95(96):1-3). Jeremiah, too, makes a prophetic announcement: "At that time Jerusalem shall be called the throne of the Lord, and they shall no more stubbornly follow their own evil heart" (Jeremiah 3:17). The prophet Ezekiel, as well, is equally clear: "Then the nations will know that I, the Lord, sanctify Israel, when my sanctuary is in the midst of them for evermore" (Ezekiel 37:28; cf. also Amos 9:11 ff.). Hence, with the coming of the Messiah, the time when the spirit of God will be poured out upon men, "all who call upon the name of the Lord shall be saved" (Joel 2:32). There are a sufficient number of such texts to constitute a sort of dawn heralding the sunrise of the full light of the New Testament, where St John assures us: "God so loved the world that he gave his only son, that whoever believes in him should not perish but have eternal life" (John 3:16). Christ now appears as the new head of the human family. Just as in Adam all men lost the life of grace, so also they recovered it more abundantly in Christ: "Then as one man's trespass led to condemnation for all men, so one man's act of righteousness leads to acquittal and life for all men. For as by one man's disobedience, many were made sinners, so by one man's obedience many will be made righteous" (Romans 5:18-19). And in the end this life of grace will blossom into divine life itself, in which the whole man will share after the glorious resurrection of the body. "Christ has been raised from the dead, the first fruits of those who have fallen asleep. For as by a man came death, so also by a man has come the resurrection of the dead" (1 Corinthians 15:20-21).

God, providence, Father of mankind

But God did not confine himself to giving man a divine destiny; he has also taken care that he himself, with the free co-operation of man, should be the very first to realise it.

He constitutes himself the universal provider, the fatherly guide of each individual and of the whole of humanity. But that is not yet all. God loves all creatures and hates nothing of his handiwork (cf. Wisdom 11:24). He is "good to all, and his compassion is over all that he has made" (Psalm 144(145):9; cf. Ecclesiasticus 18:13).

His wisdom "reaches from end to end mightily and orders all things sweetly" (Wisdom 1:8). And the author of the Book of Wisdom prays: "Thy providence, O Father, governs it for thou hast made a way even in the sea and a most sure path among the waves" (Wisdom 14:3; cf. Proverbs 16:1-9). Paul and Barnabas, preaching at Lystra to the pagans, remind them that God "did not leave himself without witness, for he did good and gave you from the heavens rains and fruitful seasons, satisfying your hearts with food and gladness" (Acts 14:17). How much more surely, then, will he guide men in the pursuit of that final and essential good of happiness for which he has destined them, by guiding them to himself? St Paul assures us that God desires the salvation of all men (cf. 1 Timothy 2:4). And there is certainly nothing purely theoretical about this desire. Saving always the free collaboration of man, God gives powerful and effective expression to this desire in giving all men the necessary grace and help for the pursuit of their happiness in him. It is for them that he sent his beloved Son to them, making him the head of the human race and accomplishing in him and through him the work of reconciling the whole of mankind with himself (cf. 2 Corinthians 5:18 ff.). Thence St Paul comes to the following rhetorical question: "He who did not spare his own Son but gave him up for us all, will he not also give us all things with him?" (Romans 8:32). In other words, if God has given us his only-begotten Son for our salvation, how can we still doubt his love, how can we doubt that he will give us lesser gifts, above all the daily aids of grace, just as he gives us our daily bread? Jesus describes himself as the good shepherd who leaves the ninety-nine sheep and goes out in search of the one sheep that has strayed (cf. Luke 15:4), as "the friend of sinners" (Matthew 11:19) who has come to call sinners (Luke 5:32), to seek and to save those who were lost (Luke 19:10). Christ assures us that our heavenly Father will welcome the prodigal son with overwhelming joy and completely reinstate him (Luke 15:20-23), and as additional assurance we are told that in heaven there will be greater joy over one sinner doing penance than over ninety-nine just who have no need of it (Luke 15:7). But here a *serious doubt* arises: if God effectively desires the salvation of men and if Christ works to this end, why are there still today two thousand million men who have not yet accepted his Gospel nineteen centuries after his redemptive death? How is it that the Catholic Church constitutes scarcely ten per cent of the human race? What is happening to the salvation of the rest? These are distressing questions for anyone who loves God, Christ and his fellow men. Although these facts form a powerful and painful incentive for all the faithful to say with St Paul: "I will most gladly spend and be spent for your souls" (2 Corinthians 12:15), in order that men may know Christ, all the same that does not allay the anxious demand of every genuine love: what is happening to *the salvation of so many men whom the Church, in fact, does not succeed in reaching?*

The Second Vatican Council has concerned itself with

finding an answer to this question. First let us look outside the *visible* confines of the Roman Catholic Church. The Church rests assured that "Those who in fact believe in Christ and have been duly baptised are in communion in a certain way, albeit imperfect, with the Catholic Church", and, notwithstanding the undeniable divergences and obstacles which are opposed to perfect ecclesiastical communion, they "are incorporated in Christ . . . and are rightly acknowledged by the faithful as brethren in the Lord" (Decree on Ecumenism, §3; cf. A.A.S. 57, 1965, p. 3). This applies to hundreds of millions of our brothers in whom, perhaps, we have never given a thought, preoccupied as we have been with the things which divide us.

There is yet a further extension in breadth of view. What is happening, we ask, to *those who do not know Christ at all*? In the Constitution on the Church, the Council replies: "Those who through no fault of their own do not know Christ or his Church but nevertheless sincerely seek God and, with the help of grace, endeavour to do his will according to the dictates of conscience, can obtain eternal salvation." Nor does this refer solely to an abstract possibility which in practice does not produce any effect. The Constitution goes on to say that they can actually be saved because God gives them the necessary help: "Nor does divine providence deny the help necessary for salvation to those who have not yet arrived at the clear knowledge and recognition of God and who endeavour, not without divine grace, to live a good life." Is there, perhaps, any proof of such aid? The Council replies, "Yes": the proof of it lies in all that is good and true which is found among them. All this is indeed the gift of God who has a care for them and guides them. "Any good or truth found among them has value in the Church's eyes as a preparation for the Gospel; it is a gift from him who enlightens every man, so that they may end by possessing life" (Constitution of the Church, §16; cf. A.A.S., 57, 1965, p. 20).

We must not imagine that the lives of hundreds of millions of men are lived out in complete separation from the influence of divine grace and that it is only because they have persevered to the last in this deprived condition that they finally become eligible for eternal life. This is not so. Through the power of the redemptive death which our divine Saviour suffered for all mankind, their whole lives are open to the assistance of divine grace in virtue of which such men are effectively enabled to work for their own salvation by following the dictates of right conscience. The work *of the Church* for the salvation of souls is certainly bound up with particular ways and means, among the chief of which are the sacraments. But God is not so bound and does not limit his activity to these means. This divine activity is unceasing, as Jesus has said: "And I have other sheep, that are not of this fold; I must bring them also . . ." (John 10:16). God certainly desires the co-operation of men but he is not limited to the collaboration of the visible organisation of the Church and to the means put at her disposal.[1]

[1] Obviously what we have said does not in any way render the missionary work of the Church superfluous. The Constitution on the Church, from which we have taken the above teaching on the salvation of those inculpably ignorant of Christ, emphasises the need for the Church's missionary activity (*loc. cit.*, no. 16). In fact, if it is true that God helps those who through no fault of their own are ignorant of Christ, it is also true that only in the Church can one find the fullness of the means of salvation of those enfeebled and wounded by original sin and surrounded by the temptations of the world through which they are exposed to the attacks of the prince of this world and the powers of darkness.

In this way, the Church and the Council enable us to envisage and understand something of God's unceasing influence on men through grace. While insisting on the duty of men—a duty imposed on them not by the Church but by Christ himself—to cling to the salvific institution founded by our Saviour, the Church also takes into account the limitations of the human work of the Church but gives due weight to the good faith of those who, through no fault of their own, have no knowledge of Christ. Far from having any egotistical and monopolistic pretensions, she fully acknowledges that the bestowal of grace is entirely in the hands of God who can give it to anyone in any way he pleases and in fact does so to those whose ignorance of Christ is not blameworthy. It could be said that in the texts from the Constitution on the Church which we have cited above, the Council opens, as it were, the eyes of the soul and of faith so that we may contemplate the prophetic vision of Isaiah in the setting of our own times, and joins with the prophet in exhorting us and the whole Church: "Arise and shine, for your light has come . . . and nations shall come to your light, and kings to the brightness of your rising . . . because the abundance of the sea shall be turned to you and the wealth of the nations shall come to you" (Isaiah 60:1, 3, 5).

The Church has a profound faith in the effects of God's work of loving providence in guiding men towards unity in herself. In her desire to work with him, she seeks to encourage her children by means of the present Declaration to co-operate also in the marvellous work of God's loving providence, all the more so because it is this work which constitutes the chief and firmest foundation of that loyal collaboration which our document commends and is hopeful of obtaining. This collaboration will endure as long as the work of God endures, that is, in the words of the Declaration, "until that time when the elect will be united in the Holy City, the city ablaze with the glory of God, where the nations will walk in its light". Working thus to achieve this ultimate goal, the Church will not exclude the realisation of more immediate ends in this world, but in the last analysis she cannot strive for any other end than that to which God's own activity is directed, the unity of the human family in Christ and in God.[1]

Religion and the unity of the human race

The aim of the Church is to promote unity among men and nations in every field of activity. Nevertheless, since she herself is pre-eminently a religious society, it is natural that her chief endeavour should be to foster harmony and collaboration with other religions and therefore to pay particular attention to what she has in common with them. No one who studies history can escape the distressing conclusion that the various religions of the world have frequently figured among major causes of discord, strife and wars. From this, the important question naturally arises: is this unavoidable or should not religion, from its very

[1] If the beginning of the passage so far commented upon should have given the impression that the Declaration refers to a *natural* unity of the human race, based on its common origin and a common natural end, these last lines should serve as a corrective. For the Church, humanity has no other ultimate end than that described in the New Testament and outlined above, and it should be abundantly clear from the concluding words of the passage that it is precisely with this supernatural happiness of man that the Church is concerned.

nature, provide, on the contrary, a particularly fruitful field, where men can meet together and hence work together in the consolidation of the unity of the human race? The document which we are discussing supplies an answer to this question by giving a phenomenological description of what men in general expect from religion:

> Men expect from the various religions answers to the profound riddles of the human condition which today, even as of old, deeply stir the hearts of men: What is man? What is the meaning and the aim of our life? What is moral good, what is sin? Whence suffering and what purpose does it serve? Which the road to true happiness? What are death, judgement and retribution after death? What finally is that ultimate and inexpressible mystery which encompasses our existence: whence do we come and where are we going?

These questionings, if compared with what has been said in the text on the spiritual foundation of unity, may cause surprise at the statement that religion is better calculated than any other factor to foster encounter among men at the deepest level. Religion indeed purports to throw light on the fundamental questions relative to the unity of the human family: man's origin, his final goal and his relation to God and to his fellow men. It should, therefore, more than anything else make for unity among men. However, this last statement immediately raises the problem: why have religions so often had the contrary effect? Even more important, what can be done to ensure that religion *may serve to unite rather than to divide men*, notwithstanding the great variety of religions existing today?

In answer to this question the document may be regarded as an example of the attitude to be taken towards all the various existing religions. The method used by the document is to seek in each of the various religions its specific contribution to the solution of man's unending questioning and to the religious needs of the human heart. Apart from this consideration of method, the purpose of the document is to define the attitude of the Church towards the great variety of religions. Hence details may be omitted and the following text cited:

From ancient times down to the present, there is found among various peoples a certain perception of that mysterious power abiding in the course of things and in the happiness of human life; at times some indeed have come to the recognition of a Supreme Being, or even of a Father. This perception and recognition penetrates their lives with a profound religious sense.

Religions, however, that are bound up with an advanced culture have struggled to answer the same questions by means of more refined concepts and a more developed language. Thus in Hinduism men contemplate the divine mystery and express it through an inexhaustible abundance of myths and through searching philosophical inquiry. They seek freedom from the anguish of our human condition either through ascetical practices or profound mediation or a flight to God with love and trust. Buddhism in its various forms realises the radical insufficiency of this changeable world; it teaches a way by which men, in a devout and confident spirit, may be able either to acquire the state of perfect liberation or attain, by their own efforts or through higher help, supreme illumination. Likewise, other religions found everywhere try to counter the restlessness of the human heart, each in its own manner, by proposing "ways", comprising teachings, rules of life, and sacred rites.

Here we will anticipate a little by giving a still more incisive example of the positive manner of considering different religions and indicating points of contact with Christianity as well as contributions to the answering of man's endless questions: it is the manner in which the Declaration deals with Islam. First and foremost the Church expresses her esteem for the Moslems "who adore the one God, living and subsisting in himself, merciful God all-powerful, the Creator of heaven and earth, who has spoken to men". After this, the various points of contact between Islam and Christianity are noted: "Though they do not acknowledge Jesus as God, they revere Him as a prophet. They also honour Mary, his virgin mother; at times they even call on her with devotion. Moreover, they look forward to the day of judgement when God will render their deserts to all those raised up from the dead. Finally, they value the moral life and worship God especially through prayer, almsgiving and fasting." The consideration concludes with an exhortation to "forget the past"—and what a past it is!—and "to make sincere efforts for mutual understanding, and so to work together for the preservation and fostering of social justice, moral welfare, and peace and freedom for all mankind".

The attitude of the Church

Here we come to the decisive question: what is the attitude of the Church—and consequently of the faithful—towards this variety of religions? Here, too, we may say that we reach the very core of the Declaration as far as its general principles are concerned. The document distinguishes between the attitude of the Church as a matter of principle and the practical procedure to be followed by the faithful.

The principles governing the attitude of the Church depend upon two equally essential elements: first of all there is the attitude of the Church in so far as the other religions are directly concerned; secondly, there is the attitude of the Church to the commandment she has received from Christ to preach his Gospel.

The attitude of the Church, as far as other religions are directly concerned, is stated in the following significant terms:

> The Catholic Church rejects nothing that is true and holy in these religions. She regards with sincere reverence those ways of conduct and of life, those precepts and teachings which, though differing in many aspects from the ones she holds and sets forth, nonetheless often reflect a ray of that Truth which enlightens all men.

Thus the attitude of the Church is characterised above all by *respect* for the rule of life and customs, the precepts and the doctrines of many of these religions, though they may differ in many ways from what she herself believes and proposes for men's belief. This respect arises from her recognition of the dignity of the human person and of what is due to it, especially in all that a man holds as most sacred, as is the case with religion; it also arises partly from a consideration of the content of individual religions, that is from the second of the two elements mentioned above, from the sincere acknowledgement of the treasures of truth and holiness contained in various religions. The seriousness and genuineness of the Church's esteem for these treasures of truth and holiness is guaranteed by the motive which prompts it. For her they are reflections of that eternal truth which enlightens every man, that is to say, they reflect the work of God in Christ. As we have seen above, when we were speaking of the spiritual foundation of unity, the Church firmly believes as a truth of divine revelation that men who profess religions other than her own were also created by God in his own image. Even though it is true that in all men God's image has been damaged by original sin, it is equally true that Christ died for all men and that, as we have seen above, God does not abandon men who, through no fault of their own, have no knowledge of him, but vouchsafes to them also the help of his grace.

We must now consider the second element on which the attitude of the Church to non-Christian religions is based, *her fidelity to the mandate she has received from Christ.*

> The Church proclaims, and ever must proclaim Christ the way, the truth and the life (John 14:6), in whom men find the fullness of religious life, in whom God has reconciled all things to himself.

Why? First of all because it is the command, from which there is no getting away, given to her by Christ, so that she can say, with the apostle Paul: "For necessity is laid upon me. Woe to me if I do not preach the Gospel" (1 Corinthians 9:16). This obligation is primarily founded on the fact that Christ died for all men without exception and has reconciled all men with God (cf. 2 Corinthians 5:14-21). The Church, however, is also moved by her solicitude for other religions since she is confident that men can find the fullness of religious life in Christ alone and of reconciliation with God which our heavenly Father has brought about through his Son and through him alone. In other words: "There is no other name under heaven given among men by which we must be saved" (Acts 4:12).

This aspect of the Church's attitude is of course likely to be the chief obstacle for the representatives of other religions and, if one may so speak, for the Church itself. Certainly we must keep in mind that the dialogue proposed by the Church in the Declaration is not specifically concerned with the differences between Christianity and other religions, that is to say, with the characteristic features of the former, but rather with the points which it has in common with other faiths with which it is hoped to engage in dialogue. Clearly, however, the Church cannot refuse to make its own specific mandate the object of dialogue and discussion and to furnish proofs of its authenticity. In spite of all this, however, it is all too easy for non-Christians to gain the impression that they are dealing with people who are insufferably arrogant and claim to be the sole possessors of the fullness of truth. The Church, too, is well aware that fidelity to her own mission inevitably exposes her to this odious suspicion. How then can we avoid this awkward situation which will certainly not help to create a favourable atmosphere for fruitful dialogue?

First of all we must point out that the Church does not

put forward her message as something which she has herself discovered as a result of her own efforts and merits, and which might justify her in claiming any superiority over others from a *human* point of view. On the contrary, she presents it as a message received from God through Christ, a gratuitous gift of God to mankind which confers no merit on the Church herself but simply makes it incumbent upon her to transmit it, not in her own name but in the name of Christ and of God. Furthermore, as far as any individual messenger charged with the duty of handing on the message is concerned, she humbly and sincerely echoes St Paul in saying: "The saying is sure and worthy of full acceptance, that Christ Jesus came into the world to save sinners. And I am the foremost of sinners" (1 Timothy 1:15).

If non-Christians should still find it difficult to understand our position, we must also point out that the Church demands nothing more from them than the attitude she herself adopts in the Declaration with regard to them: an attitude of respect involving serious consideration of the content of her message, together with readiness to admit candidly the presence of anything good or true or holy which they may succeed in discovering in it with the aid of dialogue. Lastly she asks them for genuine respect for her fidelity to the mission which she is sincerely convinced she has received from Christ.

In order to realise in practice the attitude which she commends on principle, the Church exhorts the faithful as follows:

The Church, therefore, exhorts her children to recognise, preserve and foster the good things, spiritual and moral, as well as the socio-cultural values found among the followers of other religions. This is done through dialogue and collaboration with them, carried out with prudence and love and in witness to the Christian faith and life.

So the duty incumbent upon the faithful and the means whereby they can best carry it out in their contacts with the adherents of non-Christian religions is clearly laid down. It is worth dwelling a little here on the qualifying phrase which stipulates that dialogue and collaboration should be such as to bear "witness to the Christian faith and life". This too is obvious, since it simply reflects the spirit which prompted the Church to take the initiative in putting forward the Declaration. At the same time, it serves to emphasise the source from which is derived the efficacy of dialogue and collaboration in achieving their intended purpose, namely the faith itself and the truly Christian lives of those who engage in these two activities. Therefore this qualification has important implications.

In conclusion we would stress the importance of the spirit animating the whole Declaration, as described in this chapter, for the right understanding of that part of the document which refers to the Jewish people. As far as other non-Christian religions are concerned, we trust that our remarks will serve to show that the recognition of the special relationship between the Church and the Jewish people in no way implies any less genuine esteem on her part for all non-Christian religions, or any less profound respect for those who profess them, still less any diminution in her determination to safeguard and promote all that each possesses of truth and holiness. In fact, the section of the document dealing with the Jews is simply a particular case to which its general principles are applied, as will emerge from the pages that follow.

On the other hand, the Jewish people may rest assured that the Church's Declaration of her sincere esteem for non-Christians as a whole does not in any way vitiate or minimise her very real appreciation of the special position of the Jewish people. On the contrary, it should clearly demonstrate that this recognition of the peculiar relationship between herself and the Jewish people is not a form of flattery or *captatio benevolentiae*,[1] prompted by some ulterior motive, but arises from that love of truth which governs the Church's attitude to all the non-Christian religions.

---

[1] An attempt to trap by feigned kindness (Translator's note).

III

Interlude

Before we consider in detail the very concentrated teaching contained in the Declaration on the relationship between the Catholic Church and the Jewish people, it will be as well to make a brief survey of the document's somewhat complex structure.

The Declaration owes its origin to the fact that by far the most important theme debated at the Second Vatican Council was the nature of the Church. In the course of considering this subject, the Council was naturally obliged to examine the connection between the Church and the people of Israel, with special reference to the preparatory period of the Old Testament and the earlier stages of the Church's foundation. The latter theme inevitably recalls the negative attitude adopted by a large section of the Jews towards Jesus and the Gospel. The Declaration, however, approaches this subject from a positive point of view. It seeks to show that despite all this the Jewish people is still most dear to God and that at a future time, known to God alone, all men, including the Jews, will serve him with one heart and mind.

The first deduction from this teaching is a general recommendation for the promotion of mutual understanding and esteem between Christians and Jews and the

Declaration at once proceeds to a realistic consideration of the grave secular obstacles opposed to any such development. In the first place, light is cast on the prejudices arising from the position of the Jewish people with regard to the condemnation and death of Jesus and all that then ensued. It is stated plainly that the events of Christ's passion cannot be indiscriminately imputed to all the Jews alive at the time and still less to the Jews of our own day. Consequently, the Jews should not be represented falsely as under a curse and rejected by God. The document condemns all forms of anti-semitism and demands that all sermons and instructions on this subject should be consonant with the truth of the Gospel and the spirit of Christ. At a later stage it indicates the lines to be adopted with regard to the most fundamental issue, the mystery of the cross. Indeed, the duty of the Church is to preach that Christ voluntarily submitted to his death by reason of his great love and because of the sins of *all* men and his desire to save them. The cross, therefore, must be proclaimed as the sign of God's universal love and the source of all graces.

In order to facilitate the proper understanding of all these interconnected ideas, they will be discussed under the following main headings: the beginnings of faith and the gradual building up of a chosen body among the patriarchs, Moses and the prophets; the position of the Jewish people with regard to the condemnation and death of Jesus; their position with regard to the people of God of the New Testament; the mystery of the cross; the relations of the Church with the Jewish people in everyday life.

IV

The election of Israel and the
origin of the Church

The gradual realisation over many thousands of years of
God's plan for the union and salvation of all mankind in
Christ is shrouded in mystery. The strange call to one man
out of a polytheistic people to worship the one true God
and to be led out of his own country and away from his own
people towards an uncertain future in an unknown land;
the magnificent promise that his progeny would be as
numerous as the stars of heaven, that he would become the
head of many nations, all of which would be blessed in him
—all this sounds like a beautiful eastern fable devoid of any
real meaning. Yet, as it happens, hundreds of millions of
Christians look upon this man as their spiritual ancestor and
the father of their faith while, as the Declaration points out,
hundreds of millions of Moslems also draw the inspiration
for their loyal submission to God from the faith of Abraham.
The truth that the chosen people of the New Testament is
spiritually related to Abraham is one of the chief tenets of
Christianity. It is manifestly impossible to enter into a full
discussion here of the multifarious questions raised by the
exact interpretation of the many tests in Genesis on this
subject and of the facts to which they refer. We shall simply

consider their meaning as it emerges from the New Testament and is set forth in the Declaration. From this we shall deduce their consequences.

The meaning of the calling of Abraham

Let us recall first of all the chief texts in Genesis which refer to the calling of Abram and to the promises connected with it. The Book of Genesis begins as usual by giving us his family-tree and then, somewhat abruptly, introduces the account of God's first call to him: "Now the Lord said to Abram, 'Go from your country and your kindred and from your father's house to the land that I will show you. And I will make of you a great nation, and I will bless you and make your name great, so that you will be a blessing. I will bless those who bless you and I will curse him who curses you; and in you all the families of the earth will be blessed' " (Genesis 12:1-3). As is well known, this first calling and the promises associated with it are later repeatedly confirmed in connection with the most important events in Abram's later life and are finally ratified in a formal pact. On this last occasion, to bring its importance into prominence, God changes Abram's name to Abraham: "I will make a covenant between me and you and I will multiply you exceedingly . . . you shall be the father of a multitude of nations. No longer shall your name be Abram but Abraham for I have made you the father of a multitude of nations. And I will establish my covenant between me and you and your descendants after you throughout their generations, for an everlasting covenant, to be God to you and your descendants after you" (Genesis 17:2, 4-7). Abraham and his descendants, in their turn, are to be circumcised as an outward sign of this covenant (Genesis 17:10) After the sacrifice of Isaac, this mysterious promise is once again confirmed for the last time: "And by your descendants shall all the nations of the earth bless themselves" (Genesis 22:18).

Since we cannot venture here upon a historical and critical appreciation of these texts, we will confine ourselves to what is essential, namely to the interpretation which is placed upon them under the guidance of the Holy Spirit in the New Testament, expecially by St Paul. In the Epistle to the Romans and in speaking of Christians in general, many of whom, if not the majority, were at that time non-Jews, St Paul does not hesitate to say that Abraham "is the father of us all, as it is written: 'I have made you the father of many nations'—in the presence of the God in whom he believed, who gives life to the dead" (Romans 4:16f.). Again, he writes to the Galatians: "So you see that it is men of faith who are the sons of Abraham. And the scripture, foreseeing that God would justify the gentiles by faith, preached the gospel beforehand to Abraham, saying: 'In you shall all the nations be blessed.' So then, those who are men of faith are blessed with Abraham who had faith" (Galatians 3:7-9). Evidently we are not here dealing with descent according to the flesh but according to an entirely new principle— faith like that of Abraham, whose new way of life and new prospects for the future were all founded on his faith and trust in the promises made to him by God. Here, however, another question arises. Abraham began a new life on the basis of promises made to him personally. How, then, can

Christians simply take them over and base their own lives on faith in them?

The answer to this question is to be found in the still more profound interpretation which St Paul gives in the Epistle to the Galatians of the promises made to Abraham and his posterity. In determining the exact nature of the posterity of the patriarch to which the promises refer, he writes: "Now the promises were made to Abraham and to his offspring. It does not say to 'your descendants', referring to many; but referring to one, 'and to your offspring', that is, Christ" (Galatians 3:16). Christ is, so to speak, the offspring of Abraham par excellence and it is in him that all nations will be blessed. If it is still asked how members of non-Jewish peoples can be numbered among the posterity of Abraham, St Paul replies that Christ is the link which enables the gentiles to be numbered among the inheritors of the promises. In a passage which we shall cite below, he explains that we are not concerned here with natural descent but with a connection which, as we have seen, is based on faith. Faith creates so close a union between Christ and those who believe in him that they form one mystical person with him. It is in virtue of this union with Christ that like him they become the descendants of Abraham, and therefore sharers in the promises made to Abraham and his posterity: "For in Christ Jesus you are all sons of God through faith. For as many of you as were baptised into Christ have put on Christ. There is neither Jew nor Greek, there is neither slave nor free, there is neither male nor female; for you are all one in Christ Jesus. And if you are Christ's, then you are Abraham's offspring, heirs according to the promise" (Galatians 3:26-29).

Elsewhere St Paul furnishes a further and fuller explanation. According to the Epistle to the Ephesians, God's hidden design for mankind is to "unite all things in Christ, things in heaven and things on earth" (Ephesians 1:16). From the point of view of the concrete religious situation of man at the time of Christ, this "union in Christ" means that while until then Israel alone had been the beneficiary of the promises made to Abraham and his posterity, the human situation changed completely with the advent of Christ and the revelation of the "mystery of Christ, which was not made known to the sons of men in other generations as it has now been revealed to his holy apostles and prophets by the Spirit". The secret of this mystery is that "the gentiles are fellow heirs, members of the same body and partakers of the promise in Christ Jesus through the Gospel" (Ephesians 3:4-6). The same Epistle provides further explanation with special reference to the previous condition of the non-Jewish peoples: "Remember, therefore, that at one time you gentiles in the flesh, called the uncircumcision by what is called the circumcision, which is made in the flesh by hands, were separated from Christ, separated from the commonwealth of Israel, and strangers to the covenants of promise, having no hope and without God in the world." Then comes the great change: "But now in Christ Jesus you who were once far off have been brought near in the blood of Christ" (Ephesians 2:11-13). Why has this miracle come about? Because it pleased God to reconcile to himself through Christ all things, whether on earth or in heaven, making peace by the blood of his cross (cf. Colossians 1:20). In order that God's design might be realised, Christ "our peace" has broken down the dividing wall of hostility, by abolishing in his flesh the law of commandments and ordinances (Ephesians 2:14f.), that is the old, so-called ritualistic law. And, in the words of St Paul which are quoted in the Declaration, all this is done to "create in himself one new man in place of two, so making peace, and to reconcile us both to God in one body through the cross, thereby bringing hostility to an end. And he came and preached peace to you who were afar off and peace to those who were near; for through him we both have access to the Father in one Spirit" (Ephesians 2:15-18).

Obviously a great deal more would have to be said to explain these texts in detail, but since that is not practicable here, it will suffice to bear in mind the principal idea: by the sacrifice of his life on the cross Christ, as the new head of the human race, has united in himself both Israel and the non-Jewish peoples, reconciling both to the Father. He is "our bond of peace" and has come to spread the joyful news of the peace concluded between God and mankind.

Our bond with all Abraham's descendants

Here it might be objected that although we are thus united to Abraham and to Christ, pre-eminently his offspring, that does not mean that we are united to the whole Jewish people as such, as the Declaration asserts. Nevertheless, Christ cannot be isolated from the offspring of Abraham as a whole. He is the pre-eminent offspring but not the only one. It is not without reason that God allowed two millennia to elapse between Abraham and Christ. This long lapse of time allowed for the period of long and arduous preparation which God willed. It will suffice to quote what the Second Vatican Council teaches on this point in the Constitution on Divine Revelation:

> In fact, by means of the covenant made with Abraham and with the people of Israel through the agency of Moses, God revealed himself in word and deed to the people he had thus made his own as the one living and true God, in such a way that Israel actually experienced what God's design for man was. He spoke to them through the prophets so that their understanding of him became even deeper and clearer and they made him ever more widely known among the nations (§14).

This is why the books of the Old Testament, even if they contain things which are incomplete and transitory, "still make God's teaching manifest". Since these books were the product of a living experience of God's ways with men and of his plan for their salvation, they therefore "manifest a vivid sense of God and enshrine sublime teaching concerning him. They dispense wise and salutary precepts for the conduct of our lives, they are a magnificent treasure-house of prayer and in them the mystery of our salvation lies hidden" (§15).

Since all this preparatory work looks forward to the coming of Christ and the gradual establishment of the Church, it patently concerns both the latter and the whole of the human race. In virtue of the union of every Christian with Christ, all this preparation effectively paves the way for the personal belief, calling and salvation of each individual, as St Paul affirms: "For whatever was written in former days was written for our instruction" (Romans 15:4). In this sense the Declaration cites the Church's recognition that "in accordance with the divine mystery of salvation, the beginnings of her faith and her calling are already to be found not only in the patriarchs but also in Moses and the prophets". She also acknowledges that the salvation she preaches "is symbolically prefigured in the exodus of the chosen people from the land of bondage". This is brought home to us very distinctly in the solemn liturgy of the Easter Vigil, especially in the canticle of the Exsultet. The Declaration specifically declares that "the Church cannot forget that she received the revelation of the Old Testament through the people whom God in his inexpressible mercy made the ancient covenant". It is only just, therefore, that "the Church keeps in mind the words of the apostle about his kinsmen: 'theirs is the sonship and the glory, and the covenant and the law and the worship and the promises; theirs are the fathers and from them is the Christ according to the flesh' (Romans 9:4-5), the son of the Virgin Mary". Nor is this all: "She also recalls that the apostles, the Church's mainstay and pillars, as well as most of the early disciples who proclaimed the Gospel of Christ to the world sprang from the Jewish people."

The whole of the Declaration's teaching on this point was also promulgated at the end of last year in the Constitution on the Church. According to the latter document the Church was "prefigured from the beginning of the world and the way prepared for her most wonderfully in the history of the people of Israel under the ancient covenant" (§ 2). In examining various aspects of the theme of the people of God, the Constitution observes: "He (God) therefore chose for himself the people of Israel and established a covenant with them, slowly forming them and showing himself and his designs to them in the course of their history and setting them apart for himself. All this, however, was done as a preparation and prefigurement of that new and perfect covenant which was to be ratified in Christ and of that fuller revelation which was to be manifested by the Word of God himself made flesh" (§9; cf. A.A.S., 57, 1965, pp. 6-13).

The cultivated olive tree and the wild olive branches

The foregoing clearly explains the meaning of the metaphor which the Declaration uses to state that the Church "draws sustenance from the root of that well-cultivated olive tree on to which have been grafted the wild shoots, the gentiles." This is the familiar metaphor that St Paul uses in the Epistle to the Romans, when he is explaining the relationship between the Jewish people and the members of other nations with regard to salvation. In the passage concerned, the Jewish people is compared to an olive tree planted by God himself so that it might bear fruit, a comparison which is fairly common in the Old Testament. In consequence of the refusal of many Jews to accept the Gospel (a subject to which we shall return later), God entrusted his harvest to the gentiles by offering the Gospel to them. As is recounted at length in the Acts of the Apostles, many of the gentiles did, in fact, receive it and welcome it. Applying the metaphor of the olive tree to this situation, St Paul writes: ". . . some of the shoots of the good olive tree were broken off," that is to say that many of the members of the chosen people, who were originally intended to be the first citizens of the kingdom of God, remained excluded from the new people of God because of their refusal to believe. The gentiles, on the other hand, the "wild olive shoots", who till then had been excluded from the life of the good olive in so far as they were strangers to the commonwealth of Israel and the covenants of promise (cf. Ephesians 2:12), are now grafted on to the good olive, the new people of God, and share "the richness of the olive tree" (cf. Romans 11:17), that is participate in the divine promise and in all their fruits which had been ripened during the many centuries of long and arduous preparation.

All this should suffice to dispose of a number of objections which are occasionally raised against this teaching. It is sometimes cited as an example of racism, designed to set the Jews above others in precisely that department of every man's life which he holds most sacred, namely his religion. What we have said, however, makes it obvious that this is not so. The election of Abraham, and consequently of the Jewish people, is an entirely gratuitous gift of God and is not the fruit of human genius or merits. In the Old Testament, we frequently find God speaking to the people of Israel and insisting that both the initiative and the gift were his alone:

> Do not say in your heart, after the Lord your God has thrust them (the various peoples of Palestine) out before you, "It is because of my righteousness that the Lord has brought me in to possess this land"; . . . Know therefore, that the Lord your God is not giving you this good land to possess because of your righteousness; for you are a stubborn people (Deuteronomy 9:4, 6).

It is the contrary which is true: God has persisted in his

choice of Israel in spite of its hardness of heart and many infidelities and sins. Nor did God choose Israel for its greatness, for it was the least of the nations (cf. Deuteronomy 7:7). The reason for his choice was simply this:

> It is because the Lord loves you and is keeping the oath which he swore to your fathers, that the Lord has brought you out with a mighty hand, and redeemed you from the house of bondage (Deuteronomy 7:8).

God's sovereign independence in the act of election is expressed very vividly at a much later date in the words of John the Baptist to the same people of Israel:

> Bear fruit that befits repentance, and do not presume to say to yourselves, "We have Abraham as our father"; for I tell you, God is able from these stones to raise up children to Abraham (Matthew 3:8f.).

For the same reason our document does not speak of the Church as receiving this or that *from* the Jewish people, but *through* them *from* God who is the giver of all good and the sole initiator and exclusive author of the election of Israel and of all its consequences. The Church, therefore, in recollecting all that has come down to her through Israel, is doing nothing more than recalling the wonderful works and gratuitous gifts of God.

All the same, does not the metaphor of the well-cultivated olive and the wild olive shoot suggest a *humiliation for non-Jewish peoples* and an exaltation of the people of Israel? This, too, is untenable if it is interpreted in the full context of our exposition and in the light of the fact, repeatedly affirmed in the scriptures, that the choice of Abraham and of the people of Israel was an entirely gratuitous gift of God. It is true that prior to being grafted on to the good olive tree, the non-Jewish peoples were "wild olive shoots" and strangers to the covenant of the promises of salvation. It is equally true, however, that before their election and the gratuitous gift of God's promises, Abraham and his posterity were in a precisely similar position: for them, as for all the other nations, salvation remains a wholly gratuitous gift of God. The only difference is that Israel, historically speaking, was the first people to be called and receive the promises. Even this priority, however, was purely gratuitous and was only given to Israel with a view to the salvation of all the other peoples of the world.

All things considered, however, we have good reason to maintain that the teaching in the Declaration on God's choice of Israel and all that the Church has received from God through the Jewish people, perfectly accords with the spirit of the first section of the document. All that is said of the Jews in no way detracts from the respect and esteem which the Church gladly and willingly professes for religions other than her own, or from her recognition of all that is good and holy in each of them. It is this very attitude and her love of truth which inspire her teaching on the Jewish people and its contribution to the salvation of mankind which we have set out above. All that the Declaration does is to acknowledge honestly and clearly what God has accomplished in the Jewish people and through them for the whole human race, and hence all that she herself in common with all mankind has received through Israel. At the same time it is made manifest that the initiative lies entirely with God and his sovereign freedom in the choice of his instruments for the pursuit of his work for the benefit of all men. The fruits of that work are offered to all men in Christ. Whoever benefits from them owes a debt of gratitude first and foremost to God, but also owes something to the people which God has been pleased to make the instrument of his activities. For this reason, Christians of today who visit the Holy Land in their desire to venerate the soil where Christ lived and journeyed, worked and suffered, should show profound respect for the people to whom they are bound by so many spiritual bonds and whose election and history served as a prelude to their own election and history, their own faith and salvation.

V

The Jewish people and
the actual events
of the passion

Whoever reflects on what we have had to say about the role of the people of Israel in the divine plan of salvation and on all the Church has received from God through it, is bound to ask why Christians have so often failed to act in a manner consistent with these facts. Why do they ignore the relationship inevitably created between themselves and the Jews by their very membership of the Church? Even if they are not actually hostile to the Jews, why are they uninterested in or unfriendly to them? Why has history so much that is tragic and painful to record about clashes between Christians and Jews? If we examine the historical records we shall find that on many occasions Christians have become so far blinded and that they have arbitrarily set themselves up as the avengers of Christ, discriminating against and persecuting the Jews, whom they brand as outcasts cursed by God. We are not in any way suggesting that religious motives have always and everywhere been the sole or even the principal reason for anti-semitism, especially in recent years. It has many other causes arising from racial, economic and social factors as well. It is equally undeniable that unworthy

members of the Jewish people have aroused hostility by
inflicting injustices upon Christians. We have only to think
of the persecutions undergone and denounced by St Paul
(cf. Acts 9:23-29; 13:45, 50; 14:2, 5, 19; 17:5, 13; 18:12;
20:3; 21:7; 23:12). All this last, however, refers to what
has happened to Christians. I shall not attempt to enquire
into the extent or proportions which have been assumed by
persecution and discrimination against Jews arising from
religious motives. It is not within my competence, and in
any case it would not be possible in the present context.

The religious motives which are usually adduced as a
justification for hostility and discrimination against the Jews
are well known. We shall attempt to examine their signi-
ficance and foundations in the light of the teaching of the
New Testament. Briefly stated, the indictment runs thus: as
a consequence of the unjust condemnation of Jesus, extorted
from Pilate at the instigation of the Sanhedrin, which was
the legitimate representative authority of the Jewish people,
the people became guilty of "deicide" and lost all its
privileges; the chosen people of God is no longer Israel but
the Church, the "new Israel according to the Spirit". God's
past bounty to Israel rendered it all the more worthy of
grave punishment. Israel was rejected by God and cursed, as
is shown by the great tribulations, predicted by Jesus, which
fell upon the Jewish people in the decades following the
crucifixion and culminated in the destruction of Jerusalem
and the scattering of the nation under the emperor Hadrian.[1]

---

[1] A recent author has expressed himself as follows: "In my view, it can be
legitimately said that the whole Jewish people at the time of Jesus (i.e. all those who
professed the religion of Moses) was collectively responsible for the crime of
deicide, although it was only their leaders, together with a small professional
group, who were materially involved in its perpetration." From this he concludes

In other words, the unjust condemnation of Jesus constitutes a challenge to the privileged position of the Jewish people arising from its election and former role in the preparation and realisation of the work of redemption. As a result, the Jewish people is to be regarded as frankly inferior to all other peoples from a religious point of view, precisely because it is a deicide people, rejected and cursed by God.

Here we see the problem starkly outlined in all its dramatic intensity, together with the consequences this has for the attitude of other peoples, particularly Christians, towards the Jewish people. We shall now see what must be said with regard to this point of view.

The contention described above raises two problems: firstly, the precise part played by the Jewish people as a whole in the actual sad events of the passion of Jesus; and secondly, the issue raised by the lack of faith in Christ displayed by the large majority of that people, with the consequent question of their present position in the sight of God. In this chapter we shall deal only with the first of these problems, which is already sufficiently vast and complex, leaving the discussion of the second question for the following chapter.

The accusation of deicide

Objectively speaking, there is no doubt that the condemnation and crucifixion of Christ constitutes the crime of

that "Judaism" should hold itself as "rejected and cursed by God, in the sense and with the reservations detailed above". This pronouncement is also extended to the Judaism of later times: "In this specific sense, and taking into account the biblical mentality, Judaism after the time of Christ also shares in the responsibility for deicide, in so far as it constitutes a free and voluntary prolongation of the Judaism of former times."

deicide, since according to Christian teaching Jesus was man-God. On the other hand, it is equally beyond doubt that the guilt of deicide can only be *properly* imputed to those who have committed the crime in the full and clear knowledge of the dual nature of Christ.[1] The crucial question, therefore, is this: were the leaders of the Sanhedrin and those whom they persuaded to demand the condemnation of Christ actually in possession of such full and clear knowledge? Here St Peter's famous words are very much to the point: after rebuking the Jews of Jerusalem with the words, "You killed the author of life", he adds almost immediately: "And now, brethren, I know that you acted in ignorance, as did also your rulers" (Acts 3:15, 17). St Paul echoes this in speaking to the Jews at Antioch in Pisidia:

> For those who live in Jerusalem, and their leaders, because they did not recognise him (Christ) nor understand the utterances of the prophets which are read every Sabbath, fulfilled these by condemning him (Acts 13:27).

In these statements, the apostles do no more than emulate the mildness of Jesus himself in his prayer on the cross: "Father, forgive them, for they know not what they do" (Luke 23:34). In the short space available here we cannot give an exhaustive interpretation of these texts and it must suffice to establish that they cannot possibly be regarded as

---

[1] We cannot speak of the guilt of deicide objectively in the external forum and simultaneously leave the question of possible ignorance to the judgement of God. Here we are asking whether certain *persons* can be accused of culpability for deicide or not, and the problem of their subjective knowledge or lack of it is as vital as the objective qualification of the crime itself.

completely exonerating those responsible for the death of
Jesus. There would have been no need for Christ's demand
for pardon had their ignorance been complete and their
guilt consequently excluded. On the other hand we cannot
treat our Lord's words as an empty meaningless formula.
In his prayer, Christ clearly supports his supplication for
their pardon with a genuine excuse in favour of the Jews.[1]

If there was a certain *ignorance* on the part of those who
were responsible, it obviously *primarily revolved around* a
point which it was extremely difficult for a Jew to understand, namely the *divinity of Jesus*. For centuries Jewish
people had been educated in the most rigid monotheism
and a spiritual concept of God. Hence, for a Jew the idea of
"God made flesh" and a "*son* of God" was something very
hard to comprehend, so much so that St Peter himself only
learned it through revelation from the Father (cf. Matthew
16:18). In saying this we have no desire to deny the efficacy
of Christ's own statements about his divinity or the
sufficiency of the proofs furnished for it. This sufficiency,
however, simply shows that ignorance might have been
due to prejudice and have been culpable; it does not prove
that it did not exist at all. Finally, if this was the position of
the leaders, what would have been the extent of the ignorance
of the ordinary populace? If, then, the formal guilt of
deicide cannot be unequivocally attributed to the leaders
and to those of the people who were directly involved in

---

[1] The Greek word used by St Paul is *agnoesantes*, which means both not to know
and not to acknowledge; St Peter often uses the word *agnoia* which comes from
the same verb. It is known that, in biblical language, this term denotes a mixture
of both excusable and culpable ignorance. Hence it is unjustifiable to assert that
St Peter probably used the term out of delicacy or as a legitimate means of
placating his audience, which is tantamount to saying that it is an empty formula.

the trial of Jesus, still less can it be imputed to members of the Jewish diaspora and again even less to the Jews of later times.[1]

Is the Jewish people collectively responsible?

There still remains the more general responsibility for *the condemnation of an innocent man, known as a good and holy teacher and even as a prophet,* even *the* Prophet, the promised Messiah. For our purpose it is essential to enquire whether *the whole people was involved in this responsibility, and if so in what sense.* In replying to this question it is of paramount importance to adhere faithfully to the account in the Gospels and to interpret it, not according to the mental outlook of our own time, but in the light of the outlook current at the time of the events concerned. It is equally important to avoid asserting more than is actually contained

---

[1] Although it was employed in earlier redactions, the expression "guilty of deicide" no longer appears in the final draft of the Declaration. The reason for this omission was officially explained at the Council by the President of the Secretariat for Christian Unity before the voting: "A comparison of the present text with the draft which you approved last year shows that the Secretariat proposes to remove the term 'guilty of deicide' from the text. Why? It is known that most of the difficulties and controversies arose from the use of this expression, so that it almost seemed as if the schema was at variance with the Gospel. On the other hand, it will be clear to anyone who reads the text, which you have just heard and examined, that *the ideas which we wished to express in the former text by means of this term are fully and accurately set out in the new text which is now being put to the vote.*" The ommission is simply due to practical reasons of pastoral prudence and provides no grounds for doubting the teaching proposed above.

In some quarters this prudence has been regarded as a cowardly capitulation to political pressure. This view, however, loses sight of two things:

(a) It was in every sense an obligation in charity to avoid any expression which not only could, but in fact had, led to errors and caused distress to many.

(b) In the long run it is to the advantage of the Jewish people that the Declaration should be fully understood and well received in Arab countries.

in the Gospels and in the other writings of the New Testament. What, then, is to be found in these which is relevant to our enquiry?

As a preamble, we would like to offer a few observations on one point which has been put forward as a solution to our problem but which in fact is not very helpful for our purpose. It is sometimes denied that the Jewish people as such was responsible for the condemnation of Jesus on the grounds that the Sanhedrin cannot be regarded as truly representing the people in any real sense, since its members were not elected by the people and simply belonged to a small privileged class or oligarchy. Hence the crowd which took part in the trial before Pilate formed a relatively insignificant section of the whole people and the latter cannot be involved in responsibility for the acts of so small a minority. For this reason, the savage cry: "His blood be upon us and upon our children" (Matthew 27:25) could not place the burden of responsibility on the people as a whole.

What can be said of this line of argument? The closing remark about the cry of the crowd is certainly valid; all the rest is not, because it judges the events according to modern western standards and measures them up against the yardstick of modern representative democracy, none of which has any validity for Palestine in the time of our Lord. The only proper procedure is to go to the New Testament directly and see how the facts and events are judged there. For this purpose we shall first of all assemble the relevant texts and data and then interpret them taken as a whole.

In the first place there are some striking statements from *St Peter*. In his first sermon, preached on the day of Pentecost, and addressed to the crowd in front of the Upper Room, he said:

> Men of Israel, hear these words: Jesus of Nazareth, a man attested to you by God with mighty works and wonders and signs which God did through him in your midst, as you yourselves know—this Jesus, delivered up according to the definite plan and foreknowledge of God, you crucified and killed by the hands of lawless men (Acts 2:22f.; cf. also 2:36).

Almost the same words are repeated in the same apostle's speech to the people of Jerusalem after the cure of a cripple: "You killed the author of life; but God raised him up from the dead and of this we are witnesses" (Acts 3:15). On another occasion he said to the Sanhedrin: "The God of our fathers raised Jesus, whom you killed by hanging him on a tree" (Acts 5:30).

St Stephen also spoke to the Sanhedrin in similar terms:

> Which of the prophets did your fathers persecute? And they killed those who announced beforehand the coming of the Righteous One, whom you have now betrayed and murdered (Acts 7:52).

Analogous expressions are used by *St Paul* in his discourse to the Jews of Antioch in Pisidia, which we have already quoted:

> For those who live in Jerusalem and their leaders, because they did not recognise him nor understand the utterances of the prophets which are read every Sabbath, fulfilled these by condemning him. Though they could charge

him with nothing deserving death, yet they asked
Pilate to have him killed (Acts 13:27-28).

In his first Epistle to the Thessalonians he writes of the
Jews:

They killed both the Lord Jesus and the prophets and
drove us out and displease God and oppose all men
(1 Thessalonians 2:15).

There is no doubt that while St Paul speaks primarily of
the Jews of Thessalonica and then of those at Jerusalem,
he subsequently refers to the Jews *in general* in view of the
fact that he had been persecuted by the Jews in many of the
cities and places where he had preached.[1]

Here we may pause to pinpoint a detail which is somewhat surprising. Neither when addressing the Sanhedrin,
nor in speaking to the people, does St Peter attribute the
guilt of the crucifixion *to all members of the chosen people* but
only to the inhabitants of Jerusalem. St Paul speaks of the
Jews in the third person and not of "*we* Jews", and the
same applies to St Stephen, even though he, with a wider
field of vision, refers to the persecution of the prophets in
previous generations.

Another series of texts is provided by the solemn prophecies of our Lord about the chastisement which would
fall upon Jerusalem until its destruction. Commentators on
these prophecies frequently argue that since Jerusalem is
both the capital city and the symbol of the chosen people,
it follows that the judgement of God on it also applies to

[1] Cf. Acts 9:23; 13:45, 50; 14:2, 5, 19; 17:5, 13; 18:12.

the whole nation. History shows that this judgement did, in fact, fall very heavily and decisively on the whole people, and it is maintained that this circumstance presupposes the collective responsibility and culpability of the whole people, otherwise it would be unjust. It is further argued that the extreme severity of the penalty is not commensurate with anything less than the complicity of the whole nation in the unjust condemnation of Christ.[1] Let us examine the texts in this context and see exactly what they say.

In the parable of the vineyard, our Lord tells what will happen after the murder of the owner's son: "Therefore I tell you, the kingdom of God will be taken away from you and given to a nation producing the fruits of it. And he who falls upon this stone will be broken to pieces; but when it falls upon anyone, it will crush him." The evangelist adds that when the high priests and Pharisees heard this parable they at once understood that Jesus was speaking of them and, as a result, sought to arrest him (Matthew 21:43-46). Again, Jesus explains his grief, which caused him to weep over Jerusalem, by announcing its impending destruction: ". . . your enemies will dash you to the ground and your children within you, and they will not leave one stone upon another in you"; and he gives the reason for this: "because you did not know the time of your visitation" (Luke 19:43 f.).

[1] A recent author cites the details given by Josephus of those who died and were taken prisoner at the siege of Jerusalem and concludes that such a punishment would be "wholly disproportionate and unworthy of God if, in his eyes, the responsibility for the murder of the prophets and of Jesus were only attributable to the religious leaders (and not even all of them; cf. Luke. 23:51) and a few hundred lawless ruffians at the most. Unless the whole nation was collectively responsible, it all remains an unfathomable mystery."

Our Lord looks back across the centuries when he solemnly admonishes the Scribes and Pharisees:

> . . . thus you witness against yourselves that you are the sons of those who murdered the prophets. Fill up, then, the measure of your fathers . . . Therefore I send you prophets and wise men and scribes, some of whom you will kill and crucify and some you will scourge in your synagogues and persecute from town to town, that upon you may come all the righteous blood shed on earth, from the blood of innocent Abel to the blood of Zechariah, the son of Barachiah, whom you murdered between the sanctuary and the altar. Truly, I say to you, all this will come upon this generation (Matthew 23:31-36).

In this catalogue of crime, therefore, Jesus includes the outrages which will be perpetrated on the prophets and teachers whom he himself will send in the future. Particularly noteworthy are the words "Zechariah, son of Barachiah, whom *you* killed".

What conclusions can be drawn from all these texts about the collective responsibility of the Jewish people for the crucifixion of Christ?

To give an exhaustive reply to this question would naturally demand a detailed interpretation of each individual text. Since the space at our disposal precludes this, we shall confine ourselves to emphasising those elements which *definitely* exclude the collective responsibility or culpability of the Jewish nation as a whole. In addition, we shall sketch the broad outlines of a positive interpretation of the texts as a whole. The latter should serve to make their precise meaning clearer and also to explain the point of view which lies behind them, as well as the motives underlying the judgements they express and the chastisements predicted by Christ.

One fundamental fact must first be noted. In none of the texts cited above does the speaker (St Peter, St Paul or St Stephen) include *himself* among those responsible for the crucifixion of Jesus. Their rebukes are always addressed to someone else, whether it be the Sanhedrin, the crowd involved in the trial, the inhabitants of Jerusalem or Jews in general. Now if these texts referred to a collective responsibility and guilt of the entire Jewish people as such, that is of all members of the people of Israel, then in all honesty the speakers would have been obliged to use the pronoun "we" and to include themselves. It follows that they neither envisaged nor implied a collective responsibility or guilt based solely on membership of the chosen people.

An important confirmation of this contention is found in the advice with which St Peter followed his rebuke in both of his two sermons to the crowd in Jerusalem, saying "Repent and be converted and save yourselves from this perverse generation" (Acts 2:37-40; 3:19). It is clear that he could not have given such advice if he had been thinking in terms of a collective guilt arising simply from the fact of belonging to the people of Israel. Obviously guilt of such a kind could not be removed by repentance and conversion since it is on an entirely different plain. Here we are concerned with guilt in the personal order and not with the all-embracing guilt of a whole nation. The phrase "save yourselves from this perverse generation" also points in the same direction. It suggests a guilt which in some way makes a man part of the "perverse generation" which incurs God's anger and from which he must detach himself in order to escape God's wrath (cf. Romans 1:18; 2:8; 5:9; 13:4; Ephisians 5:6; 1 Thessalonians 1:10).

Further support is lent to this interpretation by the fact that the apostles do not reproach the *Jews of other cities* with responsibility for the crucifixion in the same way as they rebuke the inhabitants of Jerusalem. If the responsibility were collective they obviously could not make this distinction. Why do they do so? Precisely because the guilt is in the personal order and falls upon anyone who in some way *associates* himself with the "perverse generation" which is primarily guilty, or who directly co-operated in the condemnation of Jesus, as did the Sanhedrin and the crowd which cried out before Pilate's judgement-seat. As far as the rest of the inhabitants of Jerusalem are concerned, it can at least be said that they failed to respond to the teaching and miracles of Jesus either through fear or for some other reasons of expediency, and that consequently they can be classed as partisans of those who opposed the will of God with violence and oppression. Generally speaking, it seems probable that the citizens of Jerusalem were guilty to this extent, since they had heard the teaching of Jesus and witnessed his miracles. The same guilt, however, cannot be attributed to those who lived at a long distance from where these events happened. In other places, such as Thessalonica for example, where the Jews also used violence and oppression in persecuting the disciples of Jesus, they are classed with the people of Jerusalem, especially by St Paul, not because they belonged to the people of Israel but because they allowed themselves to be led away by the same evil motives which prompted the inhabitants of Jerusalem.[1]

Here, then, we find ourselves involved *not* in a national-istic frame of reference, so to speak, but in an *exclusively religious* context. We are confronted with a biblical concept according to which there exist in the world powers which are hostile to God. In the prophets, especially Isaiah, these

---

[1] Here it is important to note a psychological and doctrinal idiosyncrasy which is reflected in the language used. In attributing to any individual the evil char-acteristics appropriate to a certain class of persons or to a particular person (e.g. the devil), the individual concerned is conceived as the son of that person. The following texts will make the point clear: Jesus rebukes the Pharisees thus: "You are of *your father the devil*, and your will is to do your father's desires. He was a murderer from the beginning and has nothing to do with the truth, because there is no truth in him. When he lies, he speaks according to his own nature, for he is a liar and the father of lies. But, because I tell the truth, you do not believe me" (John 8:44f.). St Paul apostrophises the magician Elymas thus in the presence of the proconsul Sergius Paulus: "You son of the devil, you enemy of all right-eousness, full of all deceit and villany, will you not stop making crooked the straight paths of the Lord?" (Acts 13:10). St John reduces the matter to a general principle: "No one born of God commits sin; for God's nature abides in him, and he cannot sin because he is born of God. By this it may be seen who are the *children of the devil*: whoever does not do right is not of God, nor he who does not love his brother" (1 John 3:9f.), which is equivalent to saying that such a one comes from the devil. This text and the whole teaching of the New Testament on the devil's role in the world and the life of man show that this concept of things has deep doctrinal roots. It is for this reason that Jesus includes the Pharisees and all those who heard him in his rebuke of the murderers of the prophets: "Zechariah, son of Barachiah whom *you* killed" (Matthew 23:35). In the same sense, St Stephen castigates the Pharisees of Jerusalem: "Which of the prophets did not *your fathers* persecute?" (Acts 7:53). Similarly St Peter, echoing the language of Jesus, includes all this world opposed to Jesus under the term "perverse generation" (Acts 2:40).

This outlook, together with the increasingly severe persecution to which the early Christians were subjected by the Jews, accounts for the special terminology frequently employed by St John, for whom the term "Jews" denotes *not* just the Jewish people but the *leaders* who opposed Jesus (cf. John 2:18, 20; 3:25; 5:10, 16, 18; 7:13; 8:22; 9:22; 10:24; 11:8; etc.). It must not be forgotten that St John wrote at the close of the first century and therefore after a whole series of very painful experiences on the part of the early Christian communities. This special usage of St John's must naturally be kept in mind lest we misinterpret what he says and conclude that he is referring to the whole Jewish people as such. We must also realise that in his Gospel the term "Jews" is *also* sometimes used in a general and neutral sense: cf. for example 2:6, 13; 7:2; 8:31; 11:55; etc.

were symbolised by the kingdom of Babylon, and later by the famous prophetic figures of Gog and Magog. This same rebellion of the kings and rulers against God is also mentioned in Psalm 2. In fact, it was precisely in this light that the Christian community in Jerusalem interpreted both the events of the passion and the persecution of the apostles by the Sanhedrin. A prayer offered by the Christians of Jerusalem, after the release of Peter and John from the hands of the Sanhedrin, begins by citing the first two versicles of Psalm 2: "Why did the Gentiles rage and the peoples imagine vain things . . . against the Lord and against his Anointed One?" and continues: "For truly in this city there were gathered together against thy holy Son Jesus, whom thou didst anoint, Herod and Pontius Pilate, with the gentiles and the peoples of Israel to do whatever thy hand and thy plan had destined to take place" (Acts 4:24-28).[1] These hostile powers, which are also designated elsewhere under the concept of the "world",[2] are, like the "perverse generation", under the shadow of God's anger, as St Paul affirms of the Jews who persecuted him (cf. 1 Thessalonians 2:14). It is for this reason that St Peter advises the people: ". . . Save yourselves from this perverse generation" (Acts 2: 40). These concepts could be still more widely explored and verified in the pages of the New Testament.

[1] These last words evidently do not mean that the powers hostile to God willingly followed the divine ordinances and designs, but that in spite of their opposition and obstruction they had in fact served his purpose in realising the designs foretold by the prophets for centuries. This passage affirms the sovereign independence of God in guiding history and the march of events even at the most critical moments and against the combined and co-ordinated forces of his most bitter enemies.

[2] Cf. Jn. 7:7; 12:31; 14:30; 15:18f.; 16:8; 17:14ff.; 1 Cor. 2:12; 3:19; 6:2; 11:32; Gal. 6:14; 1 Jn. 2:15; 3:1, 13.

The judgement which will smite Jerusalem

It is in this light also that we must see the prophecies of Jesus about the judgement which would overtake Jerusalem. In point of fact this judgement was not incurred simply and solely on account of the crucifixion; thus in the catalogue of outrages which Jesus enumerates (Matthew 23:31-36), the latter is not even explicitly mentioned. It is a punishment for "all the righteous blood shed on earth, from the blood of innocent Abel to the blood of Zacheriah, son of Barachiah" and also for that of the prophets, sages and teachers to be sent by Jesus himself. The fate of Jerusalem constitutes a sort of final reckoning at the end of a thousand years of infidelities and opposition to God. Here, too, it is *not* the fact of belonging to the people of Israel which determines the judgement but the act of opposing God and his prophets and messengers, above all Jesus.

Here, therefore, we must keep in mind the typical prophetic outlook according to which the judgement on Jerusalem is likewise a type and symbol of the universal judgement on all evil and on the powers hostile to God. So true is this that in Jesus' discourse in Matthew 24, the particular judgement of Jerusalem and the universal judgement are so interlaced that it is impossible to show where one ends and the other begins. For this reason the judgement of Jerusalem and its destruction form part of God's revelation to man whereby he makes manifest in a particular episode something of the terrible reality of the judgement with which the story of mankind will end. Since, as holy scripture tells us, this reality is of decisive importance for mankind, it is wholly consistent with the divine method of teaching to project some reflection of it into the history of man as a stern but effective and salutary warning.

Now, if this is the meaning of the terrible judgement on Jerusalem, its cause and motive are *not* the presumed collective guilt of the chosen people, but the same criterion according to which, as the scriptures tell us, God's judgements are always made and which St Paul describes in the following manner:

God will render to every man according to his works: to those who by patience in well-doing seek for honour, glory and immortality, he will give eternal life; but for those who are factious and do not obey the truth, but obey wickedness, there will be wrath and fury (Romans 2:6-8).

In other words the judgement which fell upon Jerusalem represents a verdict passed on moral and religious evil: stubborn pride, revolt against truth and the leading of a wicked life.

This double aspect of the judgement on Jerusalem—the fact that it is at one and the same time the final reckoning at the end of a whole period of history and also a type of the universal judgement to come—is not only a sufficient, but also a much better explanation of the city's actual terrible fate recorded in history that any supposed collective responsibility or guilt of the whole Jewish people for the crucifixion of Jesus. Hence there is no reason to invoke any such responsibility to account for it.[1]

It may be objected that though this is true, the judgement does not perhaps fall on all the people without distinction, a fact which nevertheless supposes a certain collective responsibility of guilt. To this we would reply as follows: the fact that the judgement affects the whole people presupposes certain social factors or bonds of such a nature that through them the leaders and the people share a common fate, for good or for ill; but strictly speaking it does not imply a sharing of guilt by the people. Proof of this is provided by the manner in which God, and therefore the apostles

[1] In support of the theory of the Jewish people's collective responsibility for the events of the passion, a recent author takes his stand on *the general principle* of "collective responsibility" for good or for evil and explains it as follows: "The entire people is held responsible, and therefore punished, for the crimes committed by their leaders in an official capacity, even when a large proportion of the people has had no part in them." He then maintains that this principle is also valid in the New Testament (in spite of the fact that its validity is denied as far back as the time of the exile in Ezekiel 18), and he attempts to prove this from our Lord's words addressed to the entire cities of Chorazain, Bethsaida and Capernaum (cf. Matthew 11:21-24); he also makes use of the texts we have already quoted in which Jesus imputes the murder of the prophets in former times to the Scribes and Pharisees and in which the destruction of Jerusalem is presented as punishment for these murders.

We have already given a general explanation of these texts and we would like here to add an explanation of the principle involved. In actual fact it is necessary to distinguish between collective social solidaritay on one hand, and collective responsibility in the strict sense on the other. Social and collective *solidarity* in good or in evil is manifested when a body of people collectively experience the good or the evil consequences of the acts of their own leaders (e.g. the consequences of the census of David described in 2 Kings 24). Collective *responsibility*, on the other hand, for good or for evil, exists when a whole people acquires merit or demerit as the result of the actions of its leaders and shares in the consequent reward or punishment. Hence in order to prove that the principle of collective responsibility in the strict sense is valid in the New Testament it is not sufficient to adduce instances in which the whole people has suffered the consequences of the actions of their leaders; it must be also shown that these consequences constitute a punishment for the guilt collectively contracted as a result of those acts. It must be said at once that the author does not provide any such proof.

also, deal with the chosen people after the descent of the Holy Spirit.

Who, in fact, after hearing the parable of the vineyard, would not imagine that after the decisive rejection of Jesus by the leaders, God would have rejected the chosen people and transferred the rewards of the kindgom of God to other nations? In the event, however, this was not so. For decades the apostles went on preaching among the Jews of Palestine, only very gradually venturing further afield and even then always addressing themselves in the first place to the Jews in the synagogues.

St Paul follows precisely the same procedure. Thus, when together with Barnabas he speaks to the Jews of Antioch in Pisidia, he states that God himself has decreed that his ministry should follow this pattern: "It was necessary that the word of God should be spoken first to you; since you thrust it from you, and judge yourselves unworthy of eternal life, behold, we turn to the gentiles . . ." (Acts 13:46). And in the Epistle to the Romans he declares that the Gospel "is the power of God for salvation to every one who has faith, *to the Jew first* and then to the Greek" (Romans 1:16).

God does not let loose the thunderbolts of his wrath without more ado: his generosity does not change. He holds out his gifts and offers them in such a manner to the various cities and to each individual in them as to provide *an opportunity for a free, personal decision and choice.* It is true that this decision is inevitably dependant on social factors and ties such as the lack of faith of the leaders, but not to the extent of nullifying freedom of decision. Here we must be clear that the passages in St Matthew's Gospel on the withdrawal of the kingdom of God from the people and of the terrible disaster which befalls it, are not to be interpreted as referring to an immediate and unique event. As is always the case with prophecies, Jesus indicates the chain of events without, however, enumerating all the links in the chain or giving any precise times or the nature of the connection between them.

If then the judgement overtakes the whole people, it does so only after the opportunity of making a personal choice and decision has been offered, although this may happen in an unfavourable social climate. Generally speaking, refusal to believe in the Gospel and in Jesus is a factor in this judgement, and so, in one way or another, is a free decision to ally oneself with the "perverse generation", with the powers opposed to God. This fact must be constantly borne in mind, and there is yet another confirmation of it. Christ directly offers the possibility of escaping the judgement visited on Jerusalem to those who have segregated themselves from the "perverse generation" and submitted to his Gospel. He tells them the signs whereby the approaching doom can be foreseen and warns them to leave the city as soon as they appear (cf. Matthew 24:16f.). And history shows that this did in fact happen.[1] Such a procedure would be inadmissible if God had intended Jerusalem's destruction as a punishment for the collective guilt of a people whose leaders had procured the condemnation of Jesus to crucifixion, a guilt acquired simply and solely by the fact of belonging to that people.

Such, then, is the scriptural basis of the brief but momentous statement of the Declaration on this theme: "Although

[1] For the way in which Christians reacted to the signs of the imminence of the siege of Jerusalem, cf. A. Fliche and V. Martin, *Histoire de l'Eglise, I: L'Eglise primitive*, by J. Lebreton and J. Zeiller, Paris, 1946, pp. 242ff. (gives the relevant evidence from Eusebius).

the Jewish authorities and their followers pressed for the death of Christ, the blame for all that happened in his passion cannot be attributed to all the Jews then alive nor to the Jews of the present day." Anyone acquainted with the historical facts and with the attitude of mind which from time to time arises among Christians, will realise the great importance for the future of this solemn declaration by the Council.[1] The best illustration we can give of this is a brief summary of the conclusions arising from the present study.[2]

[1] As is known, the text of the Declaration which was approved at its first reading in November 1964 differs from the final text in that it speaks more indirectly of the part of the Sanhedrin in the passion. This explains why the present version surprised and somewhat disturbed some of the Jewish people and also those who espoused the cause of Israel within the Council. Which of the two texts is better in itself and better suited to its purpose is naturally a question open to discussion and, in fact, was very widely discussed at the sittings of the competent Commission. The final choice and promulgation of the present text obliges Catholics to accept it as true, but not necessarily as the best of all possible texts. Personally I regard it as better than the previous text. It is true that the latter shows more consideration for the sensibilities of the Jewish people by only speaking indirectly of the part played by the Sanhedrin. It did not, however, convey sufficiently clearly to the minds of Christians what was to be affirmed and what was to be denied. In this sense also it was less effective in serving the Jewish cause. Moreover, in view of the atmosphere created by the demythologising school of exegesis, and the consequent tendency to take a relativistic view of historical facts, the previous text could all too easily foster in certain minds the delusion that, to avoid any appearance of anti-semitism, the Church had occasionally at least soft-pedalled these distressing historical facts in her preaching. The subsequent disillusionment would have been all the greater and more painful. It must never be forgotten that anti-semitism does not consist in the recognition of undeniable historical facts but in misinterpreting the facts and in drawing erroneous conclusions from them. The present text begins by establishing the facts as they are reported in the New Testament and constantly read by Christians. By clearly proclaiming the facts and at the same time denouncing erroneous interpretations of them from which the collective culpability of the whole Jewish people is deduced, the Council was performing once and for all an indispensable work of clarification and was doing it in the only way psychologically effective for Christians.

[2] Consideration of the question of the responsibility of the Jewish people for the events of Christ's passion may well lead us to a more abstract consideration of the general role played in human affairs by the solidarity which exists between the governmental and party leaders of a nation and its rank and file. Everyone finds it quite natural, for example, to benefit from the advantages obtained through

The result of the enquiry

1. The Jewish people cannot be said to be guilty of *deicide*.

2. Where the New Testament speaks explicitly of responsibility for the crucifixion of Jesus, it refers either to the Sanhedrin or to the inhabitants of Jerusalem and, apart from 1 Thessalonians 2:14ff., never of other cities. In these passages responsibility for the crucifixion of Jesus is never founded on membership of the people of Israel but on concurrence with the attitude of mind of the leaders of the people in Jerusalem. This is also true of the text from the Epistle to the Thessalonians cited above, in which the unjust persecution of the disciples of Jesus by the Jews is treated as a manifestation of such an attitude.

leaders, to boast of the glories of illustrious men and distinguished ancestors. Likewise, one often has to suffer through their fault. All this is considered natural up to a certain point and no one would make so bold as absolutely to exclude it. In the same way one is ashamed of the misdeeds committed by one's fellow citizens or nationals. It is to be noted, however, that this is only valid within certain limits of intensity and duration. Often enough, with the passing of generations and a little luck, the consequences of blunders and reprehensible behaviour are cancelled out, otherwise coexistence between groups and nations would become impossible. In addition, common sense reminds us that, in all fairness, other nations could make legitimate complaints about our own nation. Above all, however, justice demands respect and esteem for the dignity of the human person, and in particular the right of every man in the last analysis to be judged according to his *own* free decisions and his own actions. In the general sense outlined above, it would be natural to think that some discredit would fall upon the Jewish people as a whole in consequence of the action of the Sanhedrin which was the recognised legitimate, religious authority of the Jews. It is not this point of view which is suggested by the New Testament. As we have seen above, to cite only one example, the apostles blamed only the Sanhedrin and the inhabitants of Jerusalem for the crucifixion of Jesus; they never extended the blame to the Jews in other cities, unless they too showed the same spirit of violence and opposition to God and to his works (cf. 1 Thessalonians 2:14ff.).

3. The severity of the *judgement on Jerusalem* neither presupposes nor proves the existence of a collective guilt for the crucifixion attributable to the whole Jewish people. Its gravity is explained by the fact that it is the culmination of a whole history of opposition and disobedience to God, and of crimes committed against his messengers. It is further explained by the fact that it is a *type* of the universal judgement and is a divinely revealed warning to all mankind of the seriousness of that judgement.

VI

After the actual events
of the passion

At the beginning of the preceding chapter we reviewed the religious motives which are normally adduced in justification of dislike and discrimination directed against the Jewish people. Amongst these is the allegation that the Jewish people, by denying and condemning Christ, failed in their essential purpose and are now rejected by God. The majority followed the lead of the authorities in Jerusalem and rejected the Messiah and his message. Hence they are no longer the chosen people, and their previously privileged position and the gifts lavished upon them now only serve to render them worthy of all the greater punishment. To this is added the most appalling accusation of all, namely that they were cursed by God. In our discussion we rejected the alleged collective responsibility of the Jewish people for the death of Jesus and now we must elucidate the remainder of the problem. It is not sufficient to deny that God has rejected Israel; we must also determine what is its actual position in the eyes of God in view of the appalling events of the passion and the lack of faith in Christ shown by the majority of the people.

Before we tackle the core of the problem, let us first

define the spirit in which we, in common with every
Christian who wishes to live up to that proud title, must
approach it. This is all the more necessary since the question
is one of the utmost delicacy. The love of truth demands
that in discussing it we shall be obliged to say things which
a superficial observer might easily interpret as derogatory to
the Jewish people, though in fact this is not so. Furthermore,
we cannot avoid dwelling on a subject about which our
Jewish brethren are extremely sensitive. For this reason,
let us say at once that any remarks we may make are put
forward in all humility and charity.

Humility is the first and foremost requirement, and for
good reasons. If anyone should be tempted to harbour the
slightest thought or feeling of contempt for the Jews as a
result of the facts we shall set forth, we would remind him
once and for all of St Paul's warning to his non-Jewish
readers in the Epistle to the Romans: ". . . do not become
proud, but stand in awe. For if God did not spare the
natural branches (the members of the Jewish people who did
not believe in the Gospel) neither will he spare you"
(Romans 11:18, 20). Let us remember too with St Paul that
at one time "we were by nature children of wrath, like the
rest of mankind" (Ephesians 2:3) because we were once
sinners and it is only by the gratuitous and unmerited grace
of God that we have been saved. We have no cause, therefore, to preen ourselves. The example of those with whom
the Gospel found no welcome should induce in us sentiments
of humility and awe, conscious as we are of our own sins
and of the ease with which man falls into error (cf. Romans
11:20ff.; Hebrews 3:7-4:11; Matthew 8:11f.; 11:20, 24;
12:41f.; etc.).

Charity, too, demands that we should show that we are thoughtful for, esteem and wish well to our Jewish brethren. In this we should follow the example of the apostle to the gentiles who declared himself ready to make any sacrifice, even the most costly and painful, for the sake of his own nation: "For I could wish that I myself were accursed and cut off from Christ for the sake of my brethren, my kinsmen by race, the Israelites . . ." (Romans 9:3 f.).

God has not repudiated his people

We have already seen above some of the evidence which clearly shows that even after the condemnation of Jesus, God did not in any way reject the people he had chosen. On the contrary, he continued to offer them the Gospel of salvation. The apostles spent the first decades of their ministry preaching to the Jews of Palestine and when they began to go beyond its borders, they addressed themselves in the first place to the Jews of the diaspora. St Paul states repeatedly that this was in fact the rule imposed upon his ministry by God himself (cf. for example Acts 13:46). It was not God, then, who rejected his people. The fact is that the different Jewish communities in Palestine and the diaspora gradually succumbed to the influence of various social factors and ties, particularly the influence of the community at Jerusalem and of its leaders.

The actual cause of events is recorded in the Acts of the Apostles and in the history of subsequent times. One recalls, for example, this passage in the Acts: "None of the rest dared join them, but the people held them in high honour" (Acts 5:13). In this way the leaders' lack of faith indirectly influenced the general mass of the people through social pressure and convention and gradually brought them round to the leaders' point of view. This effect was accentuated when the Sanhedrin began to proceed against the apostles by means of arrests, threats, punishments, and later open persecution (cf. Acts 4:1-21; 5:17-41; 8:1-3; 9:1f.; 12:1f.; etc.). The same tactics were adopted in the diaspora, especially in connection with the preaching of St Paul, who regularly encountered the hostility of the leaders of the Jewish communities. Very often either he himself or his neophytes were subjected to persecution (cf. Acts 9:23, 29; 13:45, 50; 14:2, 5, 19; 17:5, 13; 18:12; 20:3; 21:7; 23:12).

But this is not yet all, and so one-sided a concept of the situation is too naturalistic. According to our Lord's own words, Jerusalem was destroyed because *"it did not know the time of its visitation"*. In biblical language "the time of visitation" means a time when God gives extraordinary help, quite beyond the general rule. "Behold, now is the acceptable time; now is the day of salvation" (2 Corinthians 6:2). For Jerusalem, Christ's public life was such a time—of his preaching when he spoke in a way that no man had ever spoken before (cf. John 7:46), the time of his miracles. Yet another such time was the moment of the greatest miracle of all, the resurrection, which Jesus himself designated as the greatest and most decisive proof of the authenticity of his mission: "No sign shall be given to it except the sign of the prophet Jonah" (Matthew 12:39; 16:4; Luke 11:29). In its turn, the arrival of the apostles in the synagogues of the various cities was such a time. As a result of the refusal to accept the good news, this hour of grace passed away and with it the special divine assistance which accompanied it.

Sufficient grace was always there but not in the same abundance. And if, with all this provision of grace, with all this help from above, they did not accept the faith, what hope was there that they would do so with less?

It is not God who rejects and suddenly, without more ado, sends down the lightning of his punishments. He continues to hold out the good news of salvation, even at the cost of the sufferings and persecution of his messengers, but through an unhappy chain of circumstances, strains and stresses and social influences, the members of the Jewish people again and again reject the Gospel until at last, respecting man's freedom of choice, God sends his messengers elsewhere. It is a process which lasts for several decades, during which, in widening circles, at least the leaders of each community come to their free choice and decision; and their individual members do so too.

It was in this manner that the situation which tortured the mind of St Paul and caused him endless sorrow and distress arose (Romans 9:2). Inevitably it raised the painful question: how can it be that the greater part of the people chosen by God, loved by him and overwhelmed with his bounties, still refuses to accept the Messiah and his Gospel? Can it, perhaps, be because their persistent incredulity has led God finally to reject them? St Paul categorically denies any such conclusion: in spite of everything, in spite of the majority's lack of faith, God has not rejected his people: "I ask then, has God rejected his people? By no means . . . God has not rejected his people whom he foreknew" (Roman 11:1-11).[1]

---

[1] From this apodictic statement it follows that we cannot interpret Romans 11:15 in the sense of a "temporary repudiation" of the chosen people. In point of fact, in Romans 11:15 St Paul does not use the term *apotheo* as in Romans 11:1f., but *apobole* which does not mean rejection in the absolute sense, which is precisely

A little later on he develops this theme still further when he says: "As regards election they are loved for the sake of their forefathers. *For the gifts and the call of God are irrevocable*" (Romans 28:28f.).[2] This statement does not contradict the immediately preceding one: "As regards the Gospel they are enemies of God for your sake" (Romans 11:28). This last passage simply stresses that while God still loves the people for the sake of their fathers, he holds them "as odious" because he detests the attitude to the Gospel.[3]

what Romans 11:1 goes on to exclude, but simply a way of behaviour from the practical point of view, in opposition to *proslempsis* (Romans 11:15), that is the assumption of the Jews into the Kingdom of God. In point of fact, this text does not concern the people as such, but only that section of it which does not believe and from which, for this precise reason, the Kingdom of God is taken away, together with the abundant graces which were offered to it at the "time of visitation". Hence, to conserve the clarity of St Paul's teaching, which ruled out of court the repudiation of the people, it is not proper to render the term *apobole* in Romans 11:15 by the word "rejection".

[2] In passing, let it be said that Daniel 9:26 does not contradict the teaching of St Paul which we have here exposed. It is true that in the Vulgate this passage reads: "Et non erit eius populus, qui eum negaturus est" ("and the people that shall deny him shall not be his"). This, however, is an unfortunate Latin translation of the original text which simply says "An anointed one shall be taken away, *in whom there is no fault*".

[3] A recent author maintains that the Jews (that is the religious community of those who profess the mosaic religion no matter when or where they are found) can in fact be said to be "rejected by God". He defines the concept of rejection as follows: "To speak of the rejection or otherwise of Israel cannot only mean to affirm or deny that this *community* has achieved or not achieved the earthly purpose for which God chose it." In support of his thesis he then adds the fact that the leaders of the people repudiated the very purpose of the covenant with God and from this he concludes: "The election of Israel automatically becomes purposeless and completely frustrated and there was no longer any sufficient reason for the privileges connected with it". He explains this still further by saying; "Israel's place in God's plan was 'relative' to Christ and to Christianity. Since it failed through its own fault to realise the implications of this relationship, it placed itself, by its own acts, in a state of objective 'rejection'."
With regard to this line of argument, it must first of all be noted that *the question is put wrongly*. In fact, when it is asked if Israel is rejected, in the context of the New Testament this question can only mean did God reject it or not? Just as the election of Israel is essentially a sovereign and gratuitous act on God's

St Paul is echoed in the solemn teaching of the Constitution on the Church, the most fundamental document of the Second Vatican Council, which was promulgated in November, 1964. Speaking of those "who have not yet received the Gospel" and who "stand in various relationships to the people of God", the document asserts that among these "in the first place stands the people which was given the covenants and the promises and which is the stock from which Christ took his origin according to the flesh (cf. Romans 9:4-5), a people which in virtue of its election is most dear (to God) for the sake of its fathers, for the gifts and the call of God are irrevocable (cf. Romans 11:28f.)" (§16; cf. A.A.S., 57, 1965, 20).

Here we may pause to clarify a misunderstanding which often arises in connection with these matters. From time to time one hears it said that the chosen people of God is no longer "Israel according to the flesh" but "Israel according to the spirit", that is the Church.

part, so also is its rejection. What Jesus said with sovereign authority to his disciples is equally applicable to the people of Israel: "You did not choose me but I chose you" (John 15:16). Put like this, the question is answered clearly and peremptorily by St Paul, who also adds a more profound reason: God's complete independence of his creatures which makes it impossible for any shortcomings on their part, such for instance as the Jews' lack of faith, to annul his faithfulness. "What if some were unfaithful? Does their faithlessness nullify the faithfulness of God? By no means. But God is true and every man is a liar, as it is written" (Romans 3:3f.).

Even if we accept the way in which the author puts the question, we still cannot say that the refusal of the leaders and the majority of the people to believe in Jesus "*completely frustrated*" the purpose of the election of Israel. In point of fact, St Paul proves his assertion that God did not reject his people by the very fact that, as in the case of Elijah, "so too at the present time there is a remnant chosen by grace" (Romans 11:5) from among the people which is saved. This remnant is composed of the apostles, the foundation of the Church, and the first Jewish-Christian communities. Taken together, these constitute the "holy first fruits" and the "holy root" (Romans 11:16) of the "good olive" into which the wild shoots (the gentiles) are grafted (Romans 11:17). In other words, the election of Israel cannot be said to have been wholly futile, still less completely frustrated.

What can be said of such a contention? Evidently it is true that the Jewish people is no longer the people of God in the sense of an *institution for the salvation of mankind*. The reason for this, however, is not that it has been rejected, but simply that its function in preparing the kingdom of God finished with the advent of Christ and the founding of the Church. From then on, the nature of the people of God and the way of becoming incorporated into it changed completely: the "people of God" of the New Testament is no longer confined to a single nation and is no longer propagated by descent according to the flesh but by faith. All this, however, does not in fact imply the disavowal of the election of "Israel according to the flesh". On the contrary, "the gifts and the call of God are irrevocable" (Romans 11:29). Israel remains most dear to God for the sake of its fathers (cf. Romans 11:28).

In this matter a proper balance must be kept, and we shall therefore follow the *example of St Paul*. On the one hand, the apostle to the gentiles very forcibly urges the universality of the kingdom of God: "For there is no distinction between Jew and Greek (Gentile); the same Lord is Lord of all and bestows his riches on all who call upon him" (Romans 10:12). Among those who have been baptised into Christ "there is neither Jew nor Greek (gentile), there is neither slave nor free, there is neither male nor female; for you are all one in Christ Jesus" (Galatians 3:28), all that counts is simply to be a "new creature" (Galatians 6:15). At the same time, however, the apostle also asserts that the advantage of the Jew "is great in every way" (Romans 3:1f.), and he explains this elsewhere by saying that "to them belong the sonship, the glory, the covenants, the giving of the law, the worship, and the promises; to them belong the partiarchs, and of their race, according to the flesh, is the Christ . . . (Romans 9:4 f.).

Why did the majority not believe?

How can we explain the refusal of the majority of the Jewish people to accept the Gospel? St Paul answers this question in two ways. The first indicates the immediate cause of their refusal from the human point of view, namely the idea which the Jews had formed of salvation. They claimed to work out their salvation themselves through their own works and the observance of the law, and not through faith in Jesus Christ, through whom salvation came as a gratuitous gift of God. To prove this, St Paul takes his stand on the facts:

What shall we say, then? That gentiles who did not pursue righteousness have attained to it, that is righteousness through faith; but that Israel who pursued the righteousness which is based on law did not succeed in fulfilling that law (Romans 9:30 f.).

Why? St Paul replies:

Because they did not pursue it through faith, but as it were based on works. They have stumbled over the stumbling-block, as it is written: "Behold I am laying in Zion a stone that will make men stumble, a rock that will make them fall; and he who believes in him will not be put to shame" . . . (Romans 9:32 f.).

4

That is to say, they stumbled on Christ, the cornerstone of the divine plan of salvation and of the house of God which was to be built, the Church. For those, however, who do not accept the divine plan Christ becomes a stumbling-block, a stone over which to fall, rather than the corner-stone of salvation. In explaining the matter still further, the apostle whole-heartedly admitted the good that was to be found among his people: "I bear them witness that they have a zeal for God", but he immediately adds: "but it is not enlightened" (Romans 10:2). He goes on to ascribe this to the fact that they did not submit themselves to God's plan and will:

> For, being ignorant of the righteousness that comes from God and seeking to establish their own, they did not submit to God's righteousness. For Christ is the end of the law, that everyone who has faith may be justified (Romans 10:3-4).

St Paul, however, does not stop at the immediate and so to say empirical reason. He looks deeper into the merciful plan of God and thus succeeds in throwing a consoling and reassuring light on the problem. If his own people stumbled and fell, it was not a fall from which they could not rise again; moreover, it was from their *temporary* fall that the salvation of the gentiles came (cf. Romans 11:11). Even this is not all. The apostle reveals the mysterious fact that, in God's plan, the lack of faith of his people is only *provisional* (though it may last for thousands of years):

> Lest you be wise in your own conceits, I want you to understand this mystery, brethren; a hardening of the heart has come upon part of Israel, until the full number of

the gentiles come in, and so all Israel will be saved; as it is written, "The Deliverer will come from Zion, he will banish ungodliness from Jacob; and this will by my covenant with them when I take away their sins". . . (Romans 11:25-27).

A little further on he continues:

Just as you were once disobedient to God but now have received mercy because of their disobedience, so they have now been disobedient in order that by the mercy shown to you they also may receive mercy (Romans 11:30).

The apostle concludes with the idea which we have underlined from the beginning of this chapter, namely that all men are sinners and therefore all have the same urgent need for God's mercy, although it must be confessed that he expresses it in a somewhat abstruse manner: "For God has consigned all men to disobedience, that he may have mercy upon all" (Romans 11:32).

The position of Israel in the sight of God

In conclusion we shall try to give a composite picture of the actual situation of the Jewish people in the plan of salvation following upon the events of the passion of Jesus and their failure to accept him.

No one can take from the Jewish people the honour arising from the part played in the past in the preparatory stages of the work of redemption. In addition, it is indisputable that the Church was grounded in this people and on individual members of it. Christ, the head of the Church, was the pre-eminent descendant of Abraham. From Abraham's stock came also his blessed Mother, the apostles, who were the foundation of the Church, and the first Jewish Christians who made up its earliest communities. True, the founding of the Church constituted an entirely new beginning, wholly due to Jesus Christ who founded it on his apostles, chosen and taught by him. This new start was manifested to the world by the descent of the Holy Spirit on the day of Pentecost. Nevertheless, this new commencement came from the people of the old covenant. The apostles were so very much Jews—and felt themselves to be so—that although they had an embryonic liturgy of their own in the "breaking of bread" and "the teaching of the apostles", they continued to visit the temple and to pray there and, as we have seen, for decades they preached to Jews in the synagogues (cf. Acts 2:46; 3:18; 5:20f.; 21:26; 24:12, 18; 22:17). In this way the Jewish people is, and remains, the "good olive" on to which the other peoples of the world have been grafted in order to become sharers in the divine promises made to Abraham and to his posterity. All this is true and will remain true for all time and all eternity.

Furthermore the sons of Israel, who have not yet been incorporated into the new people of God, are still very dear to God for the sake of their fathers and it is still their privilege that the Gospel and the kingdom of God belong to them in the first place: "To the Jew first" (Romans 1:16), just as they were the first to receive the messianic promises. Finally, there is God's own assurance that their lack of faith is only for a time, until the day—known to God alone, as the Declaration says—when the full number of the gentiles has come into the kingdom of God and so all Israel will be saved.

Conclusion

When we regard as a whole the interplay between God's loving mercy and the weaknesses and stubborn opposition of his creatures, endowed with the terrifying power of free decision, we cannot fail to end our consideration with the same reflection that concludes St Paul's treatment of the same problem. Side by side with the humble acknowledgement that all men are sinners and in dire need of God's mercy, Paul insists especially on the adorable mystery of the way God acts within the history of mankind:

O the depth of the riches and wisdom and knowledge of God! How unsearchable are his judgements and how inscrutable are his ways! "For who has known the mind of the Lord or who has been his counsellor". . . For from him and through him and to him are all things. To him be glory for ever. Amen (Romans 11:33-36).

VII

The mystery of the cross

In an earlier chapter, when speaking of the manifestations of anti-semitism, we referred to the distressing fact that at times certain Christians have been so blinded as to become the self-appointed avengers of the condemnation of Jesus. What psychological explanation can be found for this strange fact which, any consideration aside, is so little in accordance with the spirit of meekness and love of the very Jesus whom they purport to defend? The psychology of such an attitude of mind is certainly very complex and we cannot hope to analyse it exhaustively here. As far as its religious components are concerned it would seem that while it proceeds from a sincere subjective love of Christ it also depends upon an even greater misunderstanding of the mystery of the cross. Instead of contemplating the authentic and majestic concept of this mystery as the New Testament presents it, they think of it as a non-supernatural, humanitarian and emotional level, and in too naive a manner. They forget that Christ died for the sins of all men, including ourselves; they forget all the lofty motives which led him to die for us and which are revealed to us through the New Testament; consequently they see nothing more in this mystery than a heinous and calamitous injustice committed against Jesus by the Jews. They become incensed against the Jews contemporary with our Lord and quite naturally fall into the further error of transferring their indignation to the Jews around them, dislike them all and regard them as fit only to be despised, discriminated against and persecuted. In other words, they consider only the external and visible facts and forget the inner meaning of the spiritual teaching of the New Testament to which faith alone can give us access.

As a consequence, they fail to recall that while the events of the passion represent a grave miscarriage of justice procured by the Sanhedrin and Pontius Pilate, they also— and in a certain sense first of all—represent the realisation of God's eternal plan of salvation which was foretold from the beginning by the prophets. Jesus himself repeatedly declared that his passion and death must inevitably come about, not because of the power, the malice and the hatred of his enemies but simply because all that was written of him in the Psalms and the prophets must be accomplished (cf. for example Luke 18:31f.; 22:37; 24:25f., 44; Matthew 26:24, 31, 53f.). In the same way and following his example, the apostles also repeat that all that Herod and Pilate did together "with the gentiles and the peoples of Israel" served no other purpose than to "accomplish whatever God's hand and his plan had predestined to take place" (Acts 4:24-28).[1]

---

[1] From the fact that the passion and many of the circumstances connected with it were prophesied and that it was therefore inevitable for it to happen, it must not be deduced that those who participated in it as prime movers and instigators did not do so freely and are therefore not responsible for their own actions. God's foreknowledge does not exclude human liberty, otherwise it could be adduced as an excuse for all the criminals in history whose existence and actions were certainly foreseen by God.

The reply to the Council Declaration

Partly in order to counteract this naturalistic concept but also to complete its own exposition, the Declaration adds a positive explanation of the mystery of the passion and cross as it is seen in the New Testament. The text is as follows:

Besides, Christ out of infinite love freely underwent his passion and death for the sins of all men and in order that all men may reach salvation. This the Church has always taught and teaches still; and it is, therefore, the duty of the Church to proclaim the cross of Christ as the sign of God's all-embracing love and as the fountain from which every grace flows.

If the comparison is permissible, we may perhaps liken this conclusion to the development of Beethoven's Ninth Symphony. Having unavoidably spent a long time on sombre facts and obscure motives, the Declaration opens up vast horizons embracing all mankind and ablaze with the light of Christ's immeasurable charity and God's universal love for all men. Such a conclusion is both fitting and necessary.

The structure of the very condensed text is as follows. First comes the main theme: it is the Church's duty to proclaim the cross of Christ as a sign of God's all-embracing love and as the fountain of all graces. Next comes the justification of this contention: Christ did in fact die for the sins of all men and in order that all might attain salvation; moreover he did so, not out of necessity, but as the outcome of a free and spontaneous decision evoked by his immense love. All this is no new doctrine put forward here solely for the special purpose of the Declaration; it is a doctrine that "the Church has always taught and teaches still". For the remainder of our commentary it will be seen that nothing else will be done except to prove all this, point by point, with texts from holy scripture itself.

Christ died for the sins of all men

To anyone, then, who imagines himself to be wholly innocent and wishes to throw the first stone at the real or supposed culprits responsible for the death of Jesus, the Council recalls the fundamental truth which, as St Paul points out, belongs to the rudiments of Christian teaching: "I have delivered to you as of first importance what I also received, that Christ died for our sins in accordance with the scriptures . . ." (1 Corinthians 15:3). Moreover, our Lord himself says: "The Son of Man came not to be served but to serve and to give his life as a ransom for many" (Matthew 20:28). For the whole of mankind there is only one "mediator between God and men, the man Jesus Christ, who gave himself as a ransom for all" (1 Timothy 2:5 f.). In fact, as we saw in the preceding chapter, it pleased God to reconcile to himself through the blood of Christ all things, whether on earth or in heaven (cf. Colossians 1:20). Thus it was God himself who in Christ "was reconciling the world to himself, not counting their tresspasses against them" (2 Corinthians 5:19; cf. Ephesians 2:16).

The price paid for this reconciliation was none other than the precious life of Christ himself, as Peter reminds his readers: "You were ransomed from the futile ways you inherited from your fathers, not with perishable things such as silver and gold, but with the precious blood of Christ, like that of a lamb without blemish or spot" (1 Peter 1:18f.). The metaphor of the lamb recalls the idea of sacrifice, as it is expressed in the Epistle to the Ephesians: "Christ loved us and gave himself up for us, a fragrant offering and sacrifice to God" (Ephesians 5:2). The effect of this sacrifice is to cleanse us from our sins, as we learn from the Epistle to the Hebrews. If the material sacrifices of the Old Testament already effected a material purification, "how much more shall the blood of Christ, who through the eternal Spirit offered himself without blemish to God, purify your conscience from dead works (sins) to serve the living God" (Hebrews 9:13).

In order to give us a more vivid and real understanding of our state before the redemption, holy scripture repeatedly returns to the subject. Thus, in the famous hymn of the suffering servant, Isaiah says:

> All we like sheep have gone astray; we have turned every one to his own way, but the Lord has laid on him the indignity of us all ... He was stricken for the transgressions of my people ... the righteous one, my servant, shall make many to be accounted righteous, and he shall bear their iniquities (Isaiah 53:6, 8, 11).

St Paul offers the following explanation:

> While we were yet helpless, at the appointed time Christ died for the ungodly. Why, one will hardly die for a righteous man—though perhaps for a good man one will dare even to die. But God shows his love for us in

that we were yet sinners Christ died for us (Romans 5:6-8).

The effect of Christ's death is vividly described in a metaphor in the Apocalypse: "Jesus Christ who loved us and washed us from our sins in his own blood" (Apocalypse 1:5). The metaphor of washing follows the same line of thought which we have already encountered in previous chapters and which St Paul expresses as follows:

As one man's trespass led to condemnation for all men, so one man's act of righteousness leads to acquital and life for all men. For as by one man's disobedience many were made sinners, so by one man's obedience many were made righteous (Romans 5:18 f.).[1]

[1] The reference in our text to the basic Christian truth that Christ died for the sins of all men, might be used by some in the present context to exonerate the authorities in Jerusalem from the responsibility which we have maintained is attributable to them. It is well known that a somewhat similar passage in the catechism of the Council of Trent, composed by order of the Holy See for the use of parish priests, has in fact been interpreted in this sense at times (cf. *Catechismus Romanus ex Decreto Sacros. Conc. Trid. iussu S. Pii V, Pont. Max.*, Rome, 1726, pars I, cap. V, spec. num. 11–13; French trans., Paris, 1936).

What can be said of such an interpretation?

As far as the text of the tridentine catechism is concerned, two points are noteworthy:

(a) The catechism states that the guilt of Christians who commit grave sins is *in a certain sense* greater than that of the Jewish leaders, because the former have a far clearer knowledge of Jesus than the Jews. But the very use of the word "greater" does not exclude but confirms the existence of guilt on the part of the Jews which is described as "lesser".

(b) Later on in the same context the guilt of the Jews is explicitly affirmed.

With regard to the present Council document, it must be said:

(a) Here we are no longer in the context of the guilt of the Jewish people for the condemnation and death of Jesus.

(b) Our text follows immediately upon a repudiation of anti-semitism. There is therefore good reason to suppose that it too is in opposition to the manifestations of anti-semitism from the facts of the passion, that the Church does not look upon the passion in this way, but takes a very different view. This opposing view is then explained. It is not legitimate, therefore, to draw conclusions from our text as to the existence or otherwise of the guilt of the leaders at Jerusalem.

Christ died voluntarily out of love

Besides being the realisation of God's long-foretold plan for saving men from their sins, the cross is also the manifestation of Christ's *immense love*. Our Lord underwent his passion and death, not out of any sort of necessity but as a consequence of his own free, personal decision, dictated by his love for mankind. We have already come across evidence of this motive in the texts we have cited so far because the statements concerning the purpose of the passion and death of Jesus are intertwined with those referring to the love which forms the foundation of the plan of salvation itself and its realisation in Christ. It is appropriate, however, to examine this point a little more closely.

First of all, there is Christ's spontaneity and freedom of choice in his submission to his passion and death. This too is a result of his love, for love implies spontaneity and freedom. In this sense both these qualities shine out through the passages we have already quoted, but they are also explicitly emphasised in the Old Testament, especially in the texts referring to the sufferings of the Messiah, particular stress being laid on his meekness and resignation:

> He was like a lamb that is led to the slaughter, and like a sheep that is dumb before its shearers, and he opened not his mouth (Isaiah 53:7; cf. Acts 8:32).

Christ himself also expresses the same idea very forcefully:

> For this reason the Father loves me, because I lay down my life, that I may take it up again. No one takes it from me,

but I lay it down of my own accord. I have power to lay it down and I have power to take it again (John 10:17f.).

This liberty is both apparent and explicitly affirmed in the Gospel account of the passion. To the man who tried to prevent his arrest Christ said:

> Put your sword back into its place . . .; Do you think that I cannot appeal to my Father, and that he will at once send me more than twelve legions of angels? But how then should the scriptures be fulfilled, that it must be so? (Matthew 26:52; cf. John 7:30; 8:20).

Finally, Christ confirms his own freedom with a miracle by making all those who had come out to arrest him draw back and fall to the ground for a moment and so demonstrating once more the complete freedom of his acquiescence in his passion (cf. John 18:6).

The charity of Christ

"Christ loved us and gave himself up for us, a fragrant offering and sacrifice to God" (Ephesians 5:2). In this text there already appears a characteristic feature of the New Testament which, when speaking of the love of Christ and of God's love, does not so much rely on the verbal affirmation of that love as on the facts which manifest it. Jesus himself defined the basic principle according to which love may be judged: "Greater love has no man than this, that a man lay down his life for his friends" (John 15:13). Hence St John writes: "By this we know love, that he laid down his life for us" (1 John 3:16). And St Paul was pierced to the heart with the sense of Christ's love, when he declared: "I live by faith in the Son of God, who loved me and gave himself for me" (Galatians 2:20). For him the charity of Christ was a mystery "which surpasses knowledge" (Ephesians 3:19), and at the same time supplied the momentum behind his enormous and tireless activity: "For the love of Christ controls us, because we are convinced that one has died for all; therefore all have died. And he died for all, that those who live might live no longer for themselves but for him who for their sake died and was raised" (2 Corinthians 5:14 f.). This same love of Christ was the foundation of his unshakeable hope: "Who shall separate us from the love of Christ? Shall tribulation, or distress, or persecution, or famine, or nakedness, or peril, or the sword? . . . No, in all these things we are more than conquerors through him who loved us" (Romans 8:35, 37).

The sign of God's all-embracing love

All that has been said casts an astonishing light upon the mystery of the cross and throws it into relief as the sign of God's universal love. The whole work of the redemption flows from it and is borne up and carried on its tide. Here, too, the New Testament prefers to tread the firm ground of fact rather than to rely on words to demonstrate God's love: "God so loved the world that he gave his only Son, that whoever believes in him should not perish but have eternal life" (John 3:16). And in another place St John points out: "In this the love of God was made manifest among us, that God sent his only Son into the world that

we might live by him" (1 John 4:9). The intensity of this
love is particularly apparent from the relationship between
God and men which previously existed. It was God who
took the initiative: "In this is love, not that we loved God
but that he loved us and sent his Son to be the expiation for
our sins" (1 John 4:10). St Paul also brings home this point:
"God shows his love for us in that while we were yet sinners
Christ died for us" (Romans 5:8), since to say that we were
sinners implies that we were enemies of God (cf. 1 John 4:10).
The intensity of God's love is also made apparent from what
our salvation "cost" him, nothing less than the sacrifice of
the life of his Son: God "did not spare his own Son but gave
him up for us all" (Romans 8:32). St Paul goes on to show
that for this reason God's love is the sure foundation of all
our unwavering hopes: if God has given his own Son for us,
"will he not give us all things with him . . . For I am sure
that neither death, nor life, nor angels, nor principalities, nor
things present, nor things to come, nor powers, nor height,
nor depth, nor anything else in all creation, will be able to
separate us from the love of God in Christ Jesus our Lord"
(Romans 8:32, 38f.).

We may add that in a certain sense the love of God for
men is interwoven with the *mutual love between the Father
and the Son*. Indeed Christ says that he accepts his passion:
". . . but I do as the Father has commanded me, so that the
world may know that I love the Father" (John 14:31). At the
same time Christ accepts his suffering because he knows the
Father and therefore knows how much the Father loves
men: ". . . as the Father knows me and I know the Father;
and I lay down my life for the sheep" (John 10:15). On the
other hand, the Father reciprocates, so to speak, with grateful

love precisely because Christ has freely given his own life for men: "For this reason the Father loves me, because I lay down my life" (John 10:17).

The fountain of all graces

Here, then, lies revealed, as far as it can be for human minds and in human language, the profound mystery of the cross. From a purely natural and human point of view, the crucified Christ appears only as the victim of a grave injustice, a scandal and a folly (cf. 1 Corinthians 1:18, 23), whereas in fact he is the "power of God" (*ibid.*) because through the work of God Christ "becomes our wisdom, our righteousness and sanctification and redemption" (1 Corinthians 1:30). The cross is the *one and only hope for humanity*, as St Paul says in these words: "Far be it from me to glory except in the cross of our Lord Jesus Christ" (Galatians 6:14), or as the liturgy of Holy Week adds: "in whom is our salvation, life and resurrection" (Introit for Tuesday in Holy Week). How wonderful is the light that comes to mankind from the cross, the tangible proof that our God is not only gracious, patient and merciful but love personified, as St John tells us: "God is love" (1 John 4:8). What encouragement we find here! What better reason for a cheerful and optimistic view of the life and destiny of the human family? This love did not remain remote from man and from his history. In the incarnation, passion, redemption and resurrection of Christ, this love has everywhere entered into the history of mankind. In him God has reconciled sinful humanity to himself; in him we have access to the Father in the Holy Spirit (cf. Ephesians 2:18); "since we are justified by faith we have peace with God through our Lord Jesus Christ. Through him we have obtained access by faith to this grace in which we stand, and we rejoice in our hope of sharing the glory of God" (Romans 5:1 f.). We know that in him God has given us all things (Romans 8:32). In the light of this, pain and suffering lose their sting. In fact, "if we are children, then we are heirs, heirs of God and fellow heirs with Christ, provided we suffer with him that we may also be glorified with him" (Romans 8:17). From this St Paul triumphantly concludes: "I consider that the sufferings of this present time are not worth comparing with the glory that is to be revealed to us" (Romans 8:18). Furthermore, "We know that in everything God works for good with those who love him, who are called according to his purpose" (Romans 8:28). Hence, "we rejoice in our sufferings, knowing that suffering produces endurance, and endurance produces character, and character produces hope, and hope does not disappoint us, because God's love has been poured into our hearts through the Holy Spirit which has been given to us" (Romans 5:3-5).

Our Declaration appeals especially to preachers to see to it that in catechetical work and preaching they do not teach anything which is not in conformity with the truth of the Gospel and the spirit of Christ. The document itself gives a shining example of how this may be done and shows exactly how to present the very difficult subject of the mystery of the passion and death of Jesus, a topic on which it is all too easy to go astray. It is concerned with the most profound truths of the New Testament and with a doctrine of sublime grandeur. The contemplation of this mystery calls to mind the words which are applied to the sin of Adam in the solemn liturgy of the Easter Vigil: "O happy fault, that merited such and so great a redeemer!" So too, without denying the guilt of the Jewish leaders in Jerusalem, any more than the liturgy denies the guilt of Adam, we can still call their deed a happy fault.

Happy indeed was the fault which was the occasion for God's work of love and mercy in raising up the standard of the cross among erring men in mortal danger as the sign of God's all-comprising love for men and the source of all graces, and as St Paul says, "where sin abounds, there grace abounds still more" (Romans 5:20). And it abounds in a measure that is measureless, with the inexhaustible abundance of the infinite love for men of God, who is Father, Son and Holy Ghost.

VIII
Living and working together

During the years taken up with the preparation of the Declaration, especially in the earlier stages, it was suggested that the Council should primarily confine itself to launching an energetic and forceful condemnation of anti-semitism on somewhat similar lines to that issued by the Third General Assembly of the World Council of Churches held at New Delhi in November–December, 1961.[1] Others, however, considered it preferable to avoid a purely negative condemnatory statement and to set out in a constructive manner the connections which actually exist between the Church and the Jewish people, on the old principle that error is best countered by a positive exposition of the truth. Apart from anything else, this last decision demanded that the document should rest on a broad biblical basis. This was all the more necessary because historically speaking one of the great obstacles to good relations between Christians and Jews arises from the supposed collective guilt of the Jewish people for the condemnation and death of Christ. It was of the first importance therefore to clarify the whole matter, and at the same time to bring into prominence the very

---

[1] Cf. *New Delhi Report*, London, 1962, p. 148; see also World Council of Churches, Division of Studies, *The Relationship of the Church to the Jewish People*, Geneva, 1964, p. 34.

real and valuable relationship between the Church and the Jewish people.

Now that the ground has been cleared, it remains to summarise the practical measures necessary to develop relations between Christians and Jews in a constructive manner.

We have already touched upon various points in the course of this study and we shall now review them as a whole.

The rejection of anti-semitism

First of all we will examine the general principles which the Declaration puts forward in connection with this subject. Passing from the negative to the positive, the first thing we encounter is the rejection of anti-semitism. The passage relating to this reads as follows:

> Furthermore, in her rejection of every persecution against any man, the Church, mindful of the patrimony she shares with the Jews and led not by political reasons but by the Gospel's spiritual love, decries hatred, persecutions and manifestations of anti-semitism, directed against Jews at any time and by anyone.

In the first place we should note the very strong terms in which this passage is couched. The rejection[1] envisaged is

---

[1] With what right do we speak of the *rejection* of anti-semitism? The use of this expression is justified here because it occurs in the opening phrase of the passage we have quoted—"in her rejection of every persecution of any man"—which serves as a premise or general principle from which the rest of the statement follows. Hence, although the word "reject" does not actually occur in the second half of the passage—possibly for stylistic reasons—we are nevertheless justified in regarding it as implied, since the second section of the passage is only a particular conclusion from the opening phrase in which the Church's total rejection of any sort of persecution whatsoever is clearly stated.

universal in its application to any form of hatred, persecution or anti-semitic activity. Moreover, no exception is admitted in favour of any person or period. Further force is also given to this rejection in virtue of the motives from which it arises. It is not prompted by the hope of gaining any political advantage or by any other mundane consideration, but by two wholly spiritual motives: the dictates of the love taught in the Gospels and the Church's consciousness of the spiritual patrimony which she shares with the Jews. In short, the force of the rejection of anti-semitism is primarily derived from the wide general principles on which the rejection itself rests. It is not *solely* based on the due and just acknowledgement of what the Church has actually received through the Jews but is a logical application of the general attitude of the Church in repudiating any sort of persecution practised against anyone, anywhere and at any time. This ultimate and fundamental principle is further clinched and confirmed in the epilogue to the Declaration as a whole. We anticipate it here in view of its connection with the point we are considering at present and because it underlines another and deeper spiritual motive for the rejection of any sort of persecution, that is the fact that all men are brothers because they are all created in the image and likeness of God. This is the ultimate reason why "the Church reproves, as foreign to the mind of Christ, any discrimination against men or harassment of them because of their race, colour, class or creed.[1]

---

[1] Anyone who has given due consideration to all the many points which we have emphasised here and which add such great force to the Church's rejection of anti-semitism, will be surprised to learn that, amongst others, it was precisely this part of the Declaration which was the object of very considerable reservation in Jewish quarters. The reason for this was the fact that the word "damnat"

Religious teaching

Through her rejection of anti-semitism the Church commits the hundreds of millions of her children in all parts of the world to implement that repudiation of all its manifestations in all they do and say. This alone is no small thing. Nevertheless, it is not enough in itself to satisfy the Second Vatican Council with its keen awareness of pastoral needs. In the course of considering the most painful doctrinal issue, namely the attribution to the Jewish people of collective guilt for the condemnation and death of Jesus, the Council devoted attention to exploring possible sources of misunderstanding in this field. Hence the Council urges all "to see to it that in catechetical work and the preaching of the word of God they teach nothing save what conforms to the truth of the Gospel and the spirit of Christ".

(condemns) used in the redaction voted upon in November, 1964 was altered to "deplorat" in the final version. These reservations were partly due to misunderstanding arising from the translation of the Latin word "deplorat" by modern, etymologically similar words, for example the English "deplores", which are much weaker and more insipid than the Latin "deplorat", which should be translated by some stronger word or phrase (e.g. the Italian "*profondamente lamentare*" or the German "*tief zu bedauern*"). There were also psychological reasons. Dissatisfaction was caused by the dissappearance from the text of the stronger word which better expressed the execration which every honest man must feel for the recent and terrible crimes committed in the name of anti-semitism in Nazi Germany. It was also said that the reason given for the substitution, namely that the Church was "condemning" the doctrine rather than the practical attitude, was not convincing. As I have said elsewhere, even Catholics are not obliged to accept the reasons adduced by Council Commissions, but only the text promulgated by the Council. It will also be realised that in the complicated work of the Commissions it is not always easy to give in every case the precise reason which effectively determined the adoption of this or that amendment. In any case, as we have shown above, we are here concerned with a genuine "rejection" of anti-semitism which, as has been seen, is surrounded by so many reinforcing principles, rests on such a wide basis and is prompted by motives of such a character that the use of this or that word to describe it is for all practical purposes unimportant and does not detract from the force and weight of the arguments for this "rejection".

Here again the universality of this very trenchant exhortation is noteworthy. From the context it is obvious that the expressions "catechetical work and preaching" cover in practice every form of religious instruction, whether oral or written, as far as this depends on ecclesiastical authority. Universal, too, are the norms laid down for such instruction. Everything is to be excluded which is incompatible—not with this or that phrase, or this or that document of the Church—but simply with the truth of the Gospel and, wider still, with that unwritten law which is the spirit of Christ, the spirit of truth, of justice and of love.[1]

A final practical recommendation of the Declaration deals with the promotion of mutual understanding and esteem between Christians and Jews. It runs as follows: "Since the spiritual patrimony common to Christians and Jews is thus so great, the Council wishes to foster and commend mutual understanding and esteem. This will be the fruit, above all, of biblical and theological studies and of brotherly dialogue."

Here we are patently concerned with the application of the general principles of the Declaration to the concrete case of the relations between Christians and Jews. The

[1] Protests were raised against the omission from the schema of the formula "Let all take care that in giving catechetical instruction or in preaching the word of God they say nothing which might arouse hatred or contempt for the Jews in the minds of the faithful" and the substitution of the one we have just expounded. We may perhaps be permitted to observe that this complaint arises from an insufficient appreciation of the audience for which the Declaration was intended. The Council addresses itself primarily to Catholics and not directly to the general public. It was consequently necessary to keep in mind the psychology of these for whom the document was meant. There is no doubt that for Catholics, as for Christians in general, the rule given in the present text that teaching must in every way conform with the spirit of Christ is incomparably more compelling than any exhortation to avoid preaching hatred and contempt. For this reason the present text is of greater service to the Jewish cause.

special circumstances by which Christians share a great
spiritual patrimony provides a means more specific than the
more generic one of dialogue and well suited to promote
mutual understanding and respect between the parties: this
means is "biblical and theological studies". In order to
arrive at a fuller and more realistic appreciation of the scope
and richness of the possibilities contained in this recommendation, we shall attempt to study it in the particular context
of all that the Declaration teaches with regard to relations
which exist between Christians and Jews, as we explained
them in Chapter IV, "The election of Israel and the origins
of the Church". We preface this with a somewhat more
penetrating analysis of all that the two parties have in
common and from this we shall deduce a corresponding
programme of methods of living and working together.

Our common spiritual heritage

Let us recall very briefly what we have already seen of the
manifold strong ties which unite the Church, the people of
God of the New Testament, with the stock of Abraham.
They stretch unbroken across the ages of our common
history, from the moment of God's act of sovereign bounty
in the choice and call of Abraham to the coming of Christ.
The whole of Israel's history from its beginning to the
advent of Christ, is also the history of God's preparation for
his Church and very closely concerns each one of us who
are her members. Abraham is the father of our faith;
Israel's prophets are our prophets too; Christ, a son of Israel,
is our Saviour and our head. Mary, the Virgin Mother of

Christ and of ourselves, was a daughter of Israel. Our faith rests upon those "pillars" of the Church (cf. Galatians 2:9), the apostles, who were also sons of Israel. Each one of us is daily nourished from the sap of the "good olive tree" and we live by the promises made to Abraham and by God's revelation handed down to us by the Jewish people in the writings of the Old Testament. We see then that the bonds which bind us to the Jewish people are manifold and deep-rooted, reaching to the very heart of our spiritual life and religion as Christians. To deny them would be to deny the very foundations of Christianity. This, then, will suffice to remind us of what has already been fully set out. Here we would dwell upon a particular aspect of this situation: our daily "meeting-place", as it were, with the Jewish people, the sacred scriptures of the Old Testament. In examining the meaning of the Old Testament for us, we will take as our guide the teaching put forward on the writings of the Old Testament by the Second Vatican Council in the Dogmatic Constitution on Divine Revelation, bearing in mind that a "Dogmatic Constitution" is the most binding form of the Church's doctrinal teaching, especially when issued by an Ecumenical Council.

The meaning of the Old Testament for Christians

Christians often complain of the difficulty they experience in trying to understand and love the Old Testament in view of the very obvious differences between it and the New Testament. The Council is the first to admit that the Old Testament speaks of God in a manner consonant with the

mentality of its first readers and hence "according to the
condition of the human race before the time of salvation
ushered in by Christ" (§15). The Council therefore acknowledges that the books of the Old Testament "contain things
which are incomplete and provisional", but adds that they
"show forth truly divine teaching" (§15). The phrase
"incomplete and provisional things" calls to mind in
particular the so-called ritual laws which formed a special
part of the religious observance of the Old Testament,
including the prescriptions for "ritual" or "levitic" purification. Such practices, enriched and augmented by the tradi-
tional customs of later times, are also found described in the
New Testament. Nevertheless, the Constitution affirms that
despite these limitations "these divinely inspired books
retain their lasting value", and confirms this statement by
quoting the well-known words of St Paul: "For whatever
was written in former days was written for our instruction,
that by steadfastness and by the encouragement of the
scriptures we might have hope" (Romans 15:4). Here, then,
is the principal and basic truth about the Old Testament
which no Christian can deny.

It is necessary, therefore, to know how to read the Old
Testament intelligently, in order to be able to identify *the
permanent elements* which concern every man, particularly
every Christian.

The Constitution summarises these very valuable elements
in the Old Testament in a few brief words. After exhorting
the faithful to look upon the books of the Old Testament
with great respect and devotion, it adds the following
reason: "they express a very lively sense of God"; in them is
contained "sublime teaching about God, and wise and

salutary guidance for the conduct of life together with marvellous treasures of prayer"; finally, in them "lies hidden the mystery of our salvation" (§ 15).

The last words of this passage remind us of the most fundamental theme contained in the Old Testament, which the Constitution underlines as the most important of all, namely its account of the *economy of salvation*, the gradually progressive manner in which *God reveals himself* to the Jewish people of the Old Covenant and through them to all mankind:

> In fact, by means of the covenant made with Abraham and with the people of Israel through Moses, God reveals himself by word and deed to the people he had thus made his own as the one living and true God, in such a way that Israel might experience in its own history God's designs for men, and that by hearing him speak through the mouths of the prophets it might obtain an ever deeper and clearer understanding of them and make them ever more fully known to the gentiles (§ 14).

The plan of salvation foretold, recounted and explained by the sacred authors, is found as the true word of God in the books of the Old Testament.

The Constitution then points to the whole meaning and purpose of the plan:

> The principal purpose to which the plan of the old covenant was directed was to prepare for the coming of Christ, the redeemer of all men, and the establishment of the messianic kingdom (§ 15).

Finally, it must not be forgotten that, as the Constitution points out, the documents in which all this is related—the books of the Old Testament—are *"the true word of God"* because, as the Constitution says elsewhere, "they were written under the inspiration of the Holy Spirit" and therefore "have God as their author" (§11). This does not mean that they were simply revealed and written down to divine dictation. For their composition

> God chose men and used them, and the individual faculties and capacities with which each was endowed, so that with him acting in them and through them they wrote down as genuine authors all those things, and only those things, which he willed to be written (*ibid.*).

In the composition of holy scripture, therefore, something happened which was similar to the incarnation of the Word of the eternal Father. In fact,

> in holy scripture, while the truth and the holiness of God remained preserved intact, there is manifested at the same time the admirable "condescension" of the eternal Wisdom, in order that we may realise the inexpressible gentleness and kindness of God who, out of his fatherly care and providence for us, adapts his language to the needs and limitations of our natures. For the words of God, expressed in human language, have been made like human discourse, just as the Word of the eternal Father took to himself the flesh of human weakness and was made like to men" (§13).

From the fact that God is the first and principal author of holy scripture it follows that

> everything asserted by the inspired authors or sacred

writers must be held to be asserted by the Holy Spirit, and that the books of scripture must be acknowledged as solidly and faithfully teaching without error the truths which God wished to be committed to writing in the scriptures for the sake of our salvation (§ 11).

Christians daily draw life from the Old Testament

By now the reader will have realised the very fruitful consequences which all this teaching has for relations between Christians and Jews. "In fact," as the Constitution states, "the books of the Old Testament have been caught up as a whole in the proclamation of the Gospel" (§ 16). We are made very vividly aware of this by the sacred liturgy, especially during the seasons of Advent and Lent. Mindful of the words of St Paul that "all scripture is inspired by God and is profitable for teaching, for reproof, for correction, and for training in righteousness, that the man of God may be complete and equipped for every good work", the Church makes abundant use of scripture for all these purposes. In this way Christians also experience in their own inner lives that lively sense of God which is characteristic of the books of the Old Testament and at the same time learn of God's plan for man and of the justice and mercy shown in his dealings with men. They deepen their understanding of all this not only through the New, but also through the Old Testament. From the latter also they glean wise guidance for the conduct of their lives, just as their Jewish brethren did in the past and still do today. From the Old Testament Christians also inherit a wonderful treasure-house of prayer, especially from the Psalter which from the earliest times has been the chosen prayer-book of the Church and the means whereby she sanctifies every hour of the day by praising and adoring God in the Holy Spirit, who is the chief author of the Psalms.

It is in their use and interpretation of these books that Jews and Christians also encounter one another at the point on which they are so sadly divided in their differing concepts of the divine plan of salvation. In spite of this painful and distressing fact, however, it is true that from the very beginnings of the Church, Christians have been gradually instructed in the mystery of salvation and prepared to admit Christ the Saviour to an ever-growing intimacy in their own lives by means of the writings of the Old Testament. One has only to think, for example, of the lessons taken from the prophet Isaiah with which the Church prepares during Advent for the celebration of the feast of the Nativity, or of the readings from Jeremiah and Isaiah, especially those referring to Christ's passion, with which she instructs her children during Lent. This is only made possible by the fact that although Christians believe that Christ has already come and has fulfilled his part in the work of redemption, they *also* believe that he will come again in glory at the last day. They look forward to his second coming with a great longing because they live "awaiting our blessed hope, the manifestation of our great God and Saviour Jesus Christ" (Titus 2:13). Just as "the Spirit and the bride say: 'Come' ", so they also pray: "Come, Lord Jesus" (Apocalypse 22:17, 20). Their desire for the second coming of Christ in glory and their preparation for it find apt expression and firm support in the books of the Old Testament, especially in the Psalms and in the prophecies of Isaiah.

Such, then, are the far-reaching ties which unite Christians and Jews, and equally far-reaching too are their points of contact in everyday life, though they themselves may not realise it.[1] They live by substantially the same faith and shape their lives according to the same divine wisdom. They express their praise and adoration of God, their sorrow for their sins and their supplications in the same prayers inspired by the Spirit of God. They can both be said to follow, though in various degrees, the same course of divine instruction and education which is called the economy of salvation. Through it they come to a knowledge of the gradual revelation of the mystery of man's salvation, hidden in God throughout the ages, to long for it and to seek its realisation, though each travels towards it along a different road.

From what has been said above, it is easy to understand the paragraph with which the Constitution concludes its own teaching on the Old Testament:

God, the inspirer and author of both Testaments, wisely arranged that the New be hidden in the Old, and that the Old be made manifest in the New. For, though Christ established the New Covenant in his blood, nevertheless the books of the Old Testament with all their parts,

[1] We have no desire to minimise the difficulties arising from the exact concept of messianism, to which we have already referred. The conclusions mentioned above are prompted by the general principle enunciated at the beginning of the Declaration, namely the desire to emphasise the points upon which Jews and Christians agree. Our task is made easier by the fact that our differences do not arise from the books of the Old Testament themselves but from later interpretations of them. As a consequence both we and our Jewish brethren can read them and meditate upon them together in peace even though we, as Christians, do not forget the teaching of the New Testament in regard to them, and as Catholics the corresponding teaching of the Church.

caught up into the proclamation of the Gospel, acquire and show forth their full meaning in the New Testament and in their turn elucidate and explain it (§ 16).

The Church has taught this for a very long time and it is obvious to Christians that the books of the Old Testament cannot be understood in themselves alone but only find their full explanation in the light of the New Testament. Nevertheless it is equally important to remember that in their turn the books of the Old Testament illuminate and explain the books of the New for which they serve as a long preparation and for whose full understanding they are indispensable. Thus many aspects of Christianity are fully treated *ex professo* in the Old Testament *alone* and this teaching is pre-supposed in the New Testament and is not repeated there. Such, for instance, are its teaching on the nature of God and his attributes, its precepts for the moral life of man, and above all his life of prayer. All this goes to show to what extent the Old Testament elucidates, explains and complements the New. It also clearly demonstrates the need for Christians to keep in constant contact with the Old Testament by reading it and meditating on it, just as their Jewish brethren read it, meditate upon it and use it in their prayers and their liturgy.

The awareness of our common heritage

The Declaration, then, has every right to emphasise the extent and importance of our common inheritance. Moreover, such is its magnitude and extent that it provides great possibilities for the rapprochement, dialogue and collaboration between Christians and Jews which the Declaration desires to promote and exhorts us to promote. Obviously this is not the place to lay down a detailed programme of possible schemes to be inaugurated in this field. The ground is still too new to make a complete survey practicable at the moment. We shall have to wait for cumulative experience gradually to lay bare the various possibilities. For this reason we shall do no more than briefly mention the pertinent indications given by the Declaration, in order to point out the possible directions the work might take and the lines along which it might be expected to develop.

The first, essential task—and it will certainly be rewarding, is to *realise* how very closely and intimately we are united to the Jews and how many paths we tread as fellow-pilgrims with them in the daily practice of our religion. The mere fact of doing this is already an important advance towards that mutual understanding and respect which the Council so warmly recommends to us and which also forms the starting-point for further progress along the same road.

We must also mention another factor which tends in the same direction, and which can be reduced to the obvious principle that the more Christians or Jews come together and the more they become capable of still closer association, the more thoroughly they will understand and *live the word of God* as contained in the Old Testament in all its fullness and richness with regard to their own lives, their relationship to God and their salvation. Naturally and inevitably difficulties will arise in connection with the interpretation of certain passages in the sacred books but there is no doubt that we can go the greater part of the way together. In this

connection we would be well advised to apply the maxim of
Pope John, who said that he himself preferred to "emphasise
the things which bring men together and to go with any man
as far as possible without prejudice to the demands of justice
and the dictates of truth".[1] If we do this as far as lies in us,
there is no doubt that we shall become more and more
closely united to one another in God, and the same God of
peace will show us the way to further progress and the
means to overcome the inevitable difficulties.

Biblical and theological studies

For the task of bringing Jews and Christians together
more closely, great importance must be attached to biblical
and theological research which will serve to throw into ever
greater relief the various aspects of our common patrimony,
to clarify our difference or at least to define our respective
points of view with greater precision. It is important,
however, to state clearly and unequivocally what objectives
are envisaged in undertaking this work together. Evidently
its purpose, unlike that of political conversations, cannot
be to work out some sort of compromise. As we saw in the
third chapter, absolute love of truth remains the fundamental law for any sort of dialogue or combined studies
between representatives of different religions. For this
reason it is indispensable that each one should expound
clearly and unequivocally the whole of his own doctrine.
In order, however, that such an exchange may remain true

[1] Cf. the Allocution to the Pax Christi pilgrimage, 26 July 1961; cf. Bea, *The
Unity of Christians*, London, 1963, p. 127.

dialogue and not become a monologue, he must take into account the doctrine and above all the mentality and language of the other party. The novel element which is characteristic of dialogue and which gives it its peculiar fruitfulness comes from the effort made to understand the person one is talking with and to set forth and explain one's own doctrine as fully and as accurately as possible in order that it may be understood by the other party.

It is evident that such a dialogue requires not only a love of truth but also great humility and charity. One must not aim at triumphing over another or at proving oneself right, but simply at searching for truth and at serving one's neighbour. Experience gained in various fields (e.g. ecumenism) has shown how fruitful this slow, patient and persevering work can be for both parties. If it should seem surprising to any Catholic that we have affirmed that such a process is beneficial for *both* parties, including Catholics, we may perhaps refer to the distinction which the Council's Decree on Ecumenism makes between the fact that the Church possesses the full richness of God's truth and the fact that its members may not always live it or be in full conscious possession of it:

> The Catholic Church possesses the wealth of God's revealed truth and all the means of grace: nevertheless, its members do not derive from it all the fervent life that they should (§4).

In addition, divine Revelation contains such riches of truth as to be inexhaustible. For this reason Christ sent the Holy Spirit to the apostles and to their successors in order to guide them stage by stage and little by little into all truth during

the whole existence of the Church on earth. This is all the
more valid for individuals who can never know the whole
of revealed truth completely and exhaustively. Hence it
is always possible for any individual knowledge to improve
and to profit from any sort of contact.

Collaboration

In point of fact the Declaration does not mention collaboration in the course of its remarks on relations between
Jews and Christians, possibly because its primary purpose
was to emphasise how much closer Christianity is to
Judaism than to any other religion, on account of the very
rich and extensive common heritage which they both
share. It is this common spiritual patrimony which
determines the specific nature of the relationship of the two
faiths to each other. Collaboration, on the other hand, is
warmly recommended by the Declaration as a valuable
means of fostering good relations between religious communities in general. Nevertheless, our common spiritual
inheritance does point to a field in which collaboration
between Jews and Christians is an urgent duty and necessity,
both before God and before men. We have been given a
talent which must not be buried but must be made to bear
interest. In the Old Testament God has endowed us with a
wealth of truth and wisdom about himself, about man and
about man's highest destiny, which he wishes to be shared
by all men. No one who loves God and loves his fellow
men can ever be resigned to the fact that hundreds of millions
of men are still ignorant of these great truths and have no

share in our inheritance. The task of dispelling this ignorance has become all the more urgent in view of the spread of both theoretical and practical atheism and of the systematic opposition to all religion, both of which imperil man's hold on his most precious and sacred possession. The duty of those who have access to the treasure-house of the Old Testament is therefore all the more serious and urgent.

There is no need to insist here on the magnitude of the task, the wide scope for collaboration and the rich possibilities which this situation opens up. Our task is to bring to mankind all that God has given them in the revelation of the Old Testament, to enable them to live in accordance with it and to understand it. In the first instance, we shall do this best if we ourselves bear witness to it through living our own lives according to its precepts. To this we can then add all those other fresh undertakings which are seen to be necessary in the light of the actual circumstances.

Obviously, any such collaboration must be developed along the general lines laid down in the Declaration and must be consonant with its wider aims. It must seek the good of all mankind by fostering a wider dissemination of the knowledge enshrined in the rich spiritual patrimony which Christians and Jews already share in common. It is important also that our common effort should be made in an atmosphere of complete freedom, in absolute fidelity to the truth and in a spirit of mutual respect, esteem and good-will.

In this chapter we have seen something of the possible, and perhaps unsuspected, practical ways of bringing Jews and Christians closer together in an atmosphere of mutual respect and charity. Although it is undoubtedly most important for both parties to abjure prejudices and to realise clearly how much they have in common, it is no less essential for this new attitude to find practical expression in their daily contacts in order that it may become more firmly fixed and more successful. There could be no better means of achieving this end than combined participation in intensive efforts to share the riches of their common spiritual patrimony with others. Collaboration in the service of so great and lofty an ideal would go far to deepen their mutual understanding and love and, at the same time, it would serve to hasten the approach of that wonderful day foretold by the Old Testament in the prophecy of Zephaniah and quoted in the Declaration: "That day when all peoples will address the Lord with a single voice and serve him with one accord" (Zephaniah 3:9).

IX

All men are brothers,
and children of the
same heavenly Father

The Declaration begins by stating that its primary purpose is to foster the unity of the human race. Of course, mankind is already one in nature in virtue of the common origin of all men and their common ultimate destiny which is God himself, who in his loving care for men guides them to their final happiness in him. This magnificent prospect stretches out before us and becomes clear with the light of God's love for men as it is revealed to us in the mystery of the cross. And yet something is still missing: something which will tell us more about God, about his love for us and our particular relationship to him and our fellow men. The clue to this missing element is to be found in the Declaration's epilogue, which is dominated by two interconnected ideas: God is the Father of all men and has created them in his own image and likeness; as a consequence, all men are truly brothers.

The epilogue proceeds by three stages; first comes the affirmation of the indissoluble connection between God and mankind provided by the divine fatherhood; next, as a deduction from this, comes the assertion that all men are

equal in the dignity attaching to every human being without
exception and that any sort of discrimination based on race,
colour, class or creed and so on must be rejected as contrary
to the will of Christ; lastly there comes an exhortation to all
the faithful to endeavour by every possible means to live at
peace with their fellow men as worthy sons of their heavenly
Father.

The family of God

Taking its stand on the fact that the cross of Christ is the
sign of God's all-embracing love, the Declaration goes on to
say:

> We cannot truly call on God, the Father of all, if we refuse
> to treat in a brotherly way any class of men, created as all
> are in the image of God. Man's relation to God the Father
> and his relation to men his brothers are so linked together
> that holy scripture says: "He who does not love does not
> know God" (1 John 4:8).

This idea of God's fatherhood, or better perhaps of his
paternal goodness to men, is emphasised at the very beginning
of the document with the statement that "his providence,
his manifestations of goodness, his saving design extend
to all men". And it is Christ's cross which is the ultimate
sign of this universal love of God for men and which
manifests it in all its splendour. It is necessary, however, to
enlarge on this in somewhat greater detail and, as far as is
possible in so short a space, to say something of the in-
comparable light which is shed upon this theme by the

New Testament. In fact, the idea of the divine fatherhood and of the brotherhood of man is an essential element of the message of the Gospel.

It is the *fatherhood* of God which stands out above all. We have only to think of the very moving terms which our Lord himself habitually uses in referring to this subject. Thus when he warns us against excessive preoccupation about food and clothing, he says: "Your heavenly Father knows that you need them all" (Matthew 6:32). Again, the motive he commends to us for avoiding ostentation in our prayers and almsgiving is this: "Your Father who sees in secret will reward you" (Matthew 6:4, 6). He commands his followers to love their enemies, adding as a reason: "So that you may be sons of your Father who is in heaven; for he makes his sun rise on the evil and on the good, and sends rain on the just and on the unjust" (Matthew 5:45). This way of regarding God is so essential for Christ that in the only vocal prayer which he taught to his followers, the name by which they are told to call upon God is "Our Father who art in heaven" (Matthew 6:9; Luke 11:2). And it is in full accord with this prayer that the Declaration points out to the faithful that it is impossible for us to call upon God as our Father in our prayers and at the same time refuse to treat one another as brothers.

What exactly does this divine fatherhood imply in its fullest sense? Is it simply another way of describing the bounty, the solicitude and the condescension of God towards creatures who have nothing specifically in common with him, or does it express his love for a creature who bears a true resemblance to him, such as a son has to his father? The context in which it appears in the Declaration is that of the universal love of God as revealed in the cross of Christ and it points to the divine plan of salvation grounded in Christ. It suggests, therefore, that the conclusion of the document should also be interpreted in this framework, as does also the text quoted from St John. The conclusion, in fact, presupposes the New Testament revelation about God and about his relationship to man, a relationship which also forms the basis of St John's maxim: "He who does not love, does not know God." Further support for this view is derived from the fact that from its very beginning the Declaration is set in the context of the supernatural vocation of man and looks forward to the time "when the elect will be united in the Holy City, the city ablaze with the glory of God, where the nations will walk in its light" (§ 1). Moreover, when the Church is speaking of her attitude to non-Christian religions in a Council document primarily addressed to her own children, it is natural that she should do so in terms of the divine plan of salvation which it is her mission to preach to the world, and should present her and her children's own attitude to their fellow men in the full light of the same divine plan. All this therefore invites us to interpret the concluding passage of the Declaration in the light of the plan conceived and realised by God in Christ and of the prospect which this holds out to mankind.

According to the repeated affirmations of the New Testament, God's plan is to offer to every man, as a gratuitous gift in Christ, the possibility of becoming the adopted child of God. In fact, as St Paul tells us, God has "predestined them to be conformed to the image of his Son, in order that he might be the first-born among many brethren" (Romans 8:29), the eldest of a family of many brothers. Christ, by coming into this world, "gave to all those who received him and believed in his name the power to become children of God; who were born, not of blood nor of the will of the flesh nor of the will of man, but of God" (John 1:12f.). For this reason St John speaks of Christians as children (Greek *tekna*; Latin *nati*) of God (cf. John 11:52; 1 John 3:1f.; likewise St Paul; Romans 8:16f., 21; Ephesians 5:1; Phillipians 2:15).

Here we are concerned with a sonship which is usually called *adoptive* to distinguish it from the natural sonship which is proper to the word alone. All the same this gift must not be considered as a mere legal act and token of affection; as will be seen, it implies a true inner transformation in man which makes him like God and which transcends his human nature and is therefore called "supernatural". It carries with it, as St Paul teaches, the gift of the Spirit of God (cf. Galatians 4:7; Romans 8:15f.), and the right to become "heirs" (Romans 8:17), to share in and with Christ in God's eternal glory to which they have been called (cf. 1 Thessalonians 2:12; 1 Peter 5:10). The ultimate reason for all this is that in virtue of this adoptive sonship man becomes "a partaker of the divine nature" (2 Peter 1:4). Although the beginning of this divine glory in us eludes our human experience at present, faith assures us of it, as St John affirms: "We are God's children now; it does not yet appear what we shall be, but we know that when he appears we shall be like him, for we shall see him as he is" (1 John 3:2). This likeness to the divine nature is so real that St Paul can exhort us: "Be imitators of God therefore as befits beloved children" (Ephesians 5:1). Christ himself, telling us to love our enemies, says: "You, therefore, must be perfect, as your heavenly Father is perfect" (Matthew 5:48).

The consequences of this teaching for those who have received in Christ the power to become God's children are far-reaching. Let none of them set himself up above others and arrogate to himself titles such as "father", "master" and so on, for Jesus said: "But you are not to be called rabbi, for you have one teacher and you are all brethren. And call no one your father on earth, for you have one Father who is in heaven. Neither be called masters, for you have one master, the Christ" (Matthew 23:8-10). Thus all men who believe in Christ together form a single family of which God is the Father and all men are his children and inter-related as brothers, with Christ as the first-born among them. A little further on we shall see to what extent this principle can plainly be applied to all men.

Brotherly behaviour

From the foregoing, the views of the Declaration on the *unbreakable connection* between the divine fatherhood, with its correlative adoptive sonship, and a brotherly attitude towards one's fellow men will be abundantly clear. On this subject the beloved disciple is incomparably our best guide:

He who says he is in the light (i.e. a partaker of divine life) and hates his brother is in the darkness still. On the other hand: He who loves his brother abides in the light and in him there is no cause for stumbling (1 John 2:9-10).

Again:

> Whoever does not do right is not of God, nor he who does
> not love his brother . . . We know that we have passed
> out of death into life, because we love the brethren.
> He who does not love remains in death (1 John 3:10, 14).

Moreover, this love must be acted upon and practical:

> But if anyone has the world's goods and sees his brother
> in need, yet closes his heart against him, how does God's
> love abide in him? (1 John 3:17).

Our Lord himself is particularly insistent that if we wish
God to pardon us we must pardon our neighbours:

> For if you forgive men their trespasses, your heavenly
> Father also will forgive you; but if you do not forgive men
> their trespasses, neither will your Father forgive your
> trespasses (Matthew 6:14-15).

This teaching is so essential and characteristic a part of the
New Testament that it determines the very language
Christians use among themselves whereby they invariably
refer to one another as "brothers", and Christ and St Paul,
speaking to the faithful about their neighbours, always refer
to the latter as "brothers" (cf. Matthew 5:22; 7:3; 12:50;
18:15-21; Luke 8:21; Romans 14:10, 13, 15; Corinthians
6:6; 8:11, 13 etc.).

Finally, let us once more recall that the divine plan of
salvation in Christ is open to all men without distinction.
It is the goal appointed for all mankind by God "who
desires all men to be saved" (1 Timothy 2:4). The proof that
this is indeed the divine will lies in the fact that God our

Father and Christ our Lord have done everything necessary on their part for the realisation of this end. The death and resurrection of Christ were accomplished for the benefit of all mankind; the unceasing operations of God, of the grace of Christ and of the Holy Spirit affect all men, including those who through no fault of their own are ignorant of Christ and his Church. The Constitution on the Church explicitly teaches that the latter are not denied the continual help of God's grace (§16) which he uses to make them his children, although we can say nothing more either of the manner in which this work is brought about or of its effects. At all events, what has been said should suffice to lead every Christian to see his fellow men through the eyes of God and of Christ and to realise the sublime dignity to which every man is called in Christ, and towards which men are guided by grace in a manner which God alone knows. It is not our business to judge to what extent others may be achieving it or who does or does not. All should consider themselves brothers and treat one another as such. Otherwise we may find ourselves in the situation described by St Augustine: "*fratrem odisti et nescis*—you have hated your brother without knowing it" (*In Ps. 54*, ad 1 vers.; *P.L.* 36, 630).

Once this doctrine has been expounded, the consequences which the Declaration draws from it become immediately obvious. They potently exclude any theory or practice which denies the fundamental dignity of man and the rights that spring from it. For the same reason any unfavourable differential treatment of men or any persecution of them on account of their race, colour, class or creed is contrary to the spirit and will of Christ.

In the light of this doctrine of the fatherhood of God and

the brotherhood of man, the full and precise meaning of the final exhortation which the Declaration addresses to the faithful is equally apparent. When the Council admonishes them to live in peace with all men—naturally as far as this depends on them—this advice is obviously intended to be interpreted in the widest and most unrestricted sense of the words. It is not simply a question of avoiding conflict but of behaving in a manner befitting the children of our heavenly Father, "who makes his sun rise on the evil and on the good, and sends rain on the just and on the unjust" (Matthew 5:45); it is a question of an all-embracing, practical love of mankind, no matter what attitude others may adopt towards that love.

An epilogue worthy of the Declaration

In conclusion, it may fairly be said that it would have been difficult to find a more appropriate conclusion to the Declaration—one that will produce the desired effect. The doctrine that mankind is truly a single family of which God is the Father and in which all men are united without distinction as brothers, throws light in a new and clinching way on the purpose of the Declaration and on the unity of the human race which it desires to serve and promote. It also makes it quite clear that with this Declaration the Council is not pursuing any particular, still less any one-sided ends in favour of this or that nation, but is concerned solely with the good of humanity at large and with the final destiny of mankind. At the same time this doctrine also casts light on the true and ultimate purpose of the election of Israel and demonstrates how great and marvellous are the "blessings" which all peoples of all times receive in Abraham, and above all in him who is the descendant of Abraham par excellence, namely Christ our Lord. For this reason nothing finer and more complimentary can be said of the Jewish people than that it was chosen to be the intermediary—only an intermediary, it is true, but a real one—for the transmission through Christ, the foremost of Abraham's progeny, of so great a divine blessing to the whole human race. Although our debt is primarily to the immense love and mercy of God we are not without obligation to the people which was chosen to be the channel of his bounty. In this light, we cannot but look upon the prejudice and discrimination detrimental to the Jewish people as all the more heinous, and it becomes correspondingly urgent and imperative to overcome them. And because they are probably some of the most powerful prejudices that have ever existed between religions, the initiative which the Council has taken in this matter and brought to a conclusion, in spite of great difficulties and very tough opposition, in order to enlighten men's minds and help to overcome them, already constitutes a shining example of the general attitude which the Council looks forward to and inculcates in this document. It is also an effective encouragement to do likewise in all the other possible fields—and they are legion—in order to eliminate antipathies and discrimination and to promote unity and charity.

The Church intends, in this way, faithfully to continue the work of her head and spouse, the prince of peace, who by his cross has made one man of both Jew and gentile in himself, bringing peace by making himself our peace (cf. Ephesians 2:14-16). Under his sway, as the Psalmist foresaw, "In his days righteousness will flourish and peace abound, till the moon be no more" (Psalm 71(72):7) or, as Isaiah said, "He shall judge between the nations, and shall decide for many peoples; and they shall beat their swords into plough-shares, and their spears into pruning hooks; nations shall not lift up sword against nation, neither shall they learn war any more" (Isaiah 2:4), because, as the same prophet says elsewhere, "the earth shall be full of the knowledge of the Lord as the waters cover the sea" (Isaiah 11:9). It is true that this enchanting prospect of a new human race refers first and foremost to the glorious advent of the messianic kingdom when, as the Declaration expresses it, "the elect will be united in the holy city, the city ablaze with the glory of God, and the nations will walk in his light". But it is also true that the way to this must be paved by degrees here below according to the general law that man must labour for his salvation here on earth (cf. Philippians 2:12) and thus prepare for the final union in Paradise. For this reason the Church herself follows, and exhorts the faithful to follow, in the footsteps of the Son of God, the prince of peace. He has shown us how those who wish to be worthy children of the God of peace must conduct themselves and has also revealed to us the happiness—than which there is no greater—of being and behaving as worthy sons of so great a Father.

Appendix 1

The text of the Declaration on the Relation of the Church to Non-Christian Religions

Paul, Bishop
Servant of the Servants of God
Together with the Fathers of the Sacred Council
For everlasting memory

Declaration
on the relation of the Church
to non-Christian Religions
28 October, 1965

1. *Preamble*

In our time, when *the human race* is being drawn ever closer together, and the ties between different peoples are becoming stronger, the Church is giving closer attention to her relationships to non-Christian religions. In her task of fostering unity and love among men, indeed among peoples, she considers above all in this Declaration what men have in common and what draws them towards fellowship.

One is the comunity of all peoples, one their origin, for God made the whole human race to live on all the face of the earth.[1] One also is their final goal, God. His providence, his manifestations of goodness, his saving design extend to all men,[2] until that time when the elect will be united in the Holy City, the city ablaze with the glory of God, where the nations will walk in its light.[3]

Men expect from the various religions answers to the profound riddle of the human condition which today, even as of old, deeply stir the hearts of men: What is man? What is the meaning, the aim of our life? What is moral good, what sin? Whence suffering and what purpose does it serve? Which is the road to true happiness? What are death, judgement and retribution after death? What, finally, is that ultimate inexpressible mystery which encompasses our existence: whence do we come, and where are we going?

2. *The different non-Christian Religions*

From ancient times down to the present, there is found among various peoples a certain perception of that mysterious power abiding in the course of nature and in the happenings of human life; at times some indeed have come to the recognition of a Supreme Being, or even of a Father. This perception and recognition penetrates their lives with a profound religious sense.

Religions, however, that are bound up with an advanced culture have struggled to answer the same questions by means of more refined concepts and a more developed

---

[1] Cf. Acts 17:26.
[2] Cf. Wisdom 8:1; Acts 14:17; Romans 2:6–7; 1 Timothy 2:4.
[3] Cf. Apocalypse 21:23 f.

language. Thus in Hinduism, men contemplate the divine mystery and express it through an inexhaustible abundance of myths and through searching philosophical inquiry. They seek freedom from the anguish of our human condition either through ascetical practices or profound meditation or a flight to God with love and trust. Buddhism, in its various forms, realises the radical insufficiency of this changeable world; it teaches a way by which men, in a devout and confident spirit, may be able either to acquire the state of perfect liberation, or attain, by their own efforts or through higher help, supreme illumination. Likewise, other religions found everywhere try to counter the restlessness of the human heart, each in its own manner, by proposing "ways", comprising teachings, rules of life, and sacred rites.

The Catholic Church rejects nothing that is true and holy in these religions. She regards with sincere reverence those ways of conduct and of life, those precepts and teachings which, though differing in many aspects from the ones she holds and sets forth, nonetheless often reflect a ray of that Truth which enlightens all men. Indeed, the Church proclaims, and ever must proclaim Christ, "the way, the truth, and the life" (John 14:6), in whom men may find the fulness of religious life, in whom God has reconciled all things to himself.[1]

The Church therefore exhorts her children to recognise, preserve and foster the good things, spiritual and moral, as well as the socio-cultural values found among the followers of other religions. This is done through dialogue and collaboration with them, carried out with prudence and love and in witness to the christian faith and life.

[1] Cf. 2 Corinthians 5:18–19.

3. Islam

The Church regards with esteem also the Moslems. They adore the one God, living and subsisting in himself, merciful and all-powerful, the Creator of heaven and earth,[1] who has spoken to men; they take pains to submit wholeheartedly to even his inscrutable decrees, just as Abraham, with whom the faith of Islam is gladly linked, submitted to God. Though they do not acknowledge Jesus as God, they revere him as a prophet. They also honour Mary his virgin mother; at times they even call on her with devotion. Moreover, they look forward to the day of judgement when God will render their deserts to all those raised up from the dead. Finally, they value the moral life and worship God especially through prayer, almsgiving and fasting.

In the course of centuries there have indeed been many quarrels and hostilities between Christians and Moslems. But now the Council exhorts everyone to forget the past, to make sincere efforts for mutual understanding, and so to work together for the preservation and fostering of social justice, moral welfare, and peace and freedom for all mankind.

4. Judaism

As the Council searches into the mystery of the Church, it remembers the bond which spiritually ties the people of the New Covenant to the offspring of Abraham.

[1] Cf. Gregory VII, Letter XXI to Anzio (Nacir), king of Mauritania (p. 148, col. 450f.)

Thus the Church acknowledges that the beginnings of her faith and her election, according to God's saving design, are found already in the Patriarchs, Moses and the prophets. She professes that all who believe in Christ—Abraham's sons according to the faith[1]—are included in the same Patriarch's call, and likewise that the salvation of the Church is symbolically prefigured in the exodus of the chosen people from the land of bondage. The Church, therefore, cannot forget that she received the revelation of the Old Testament through the people with whom God in his inexpressible mercy made the Ancient Covenant. Nor can she forget that she draws sustenance from the root of that well-cultivated olive tree onto which have been grafted the wild shoots, the Gentiles.[2] Indeed, the Church believes that by his cross Christ our Peace reconciled Jews and Gentiles, making both one in himself.[3]

The Church keeps ever in mind the words of the Apostle about his kinsmen: "theirs is the sonship and the glory and the covenant and the law and the worship and the promises; theirs are the fathers and from them is the Christ according to the flesh" (Romans 9:4-5), the Son of the Virgin Mary. She also recalls that the Apostles, the Church's mainstay and pillars, as well as most of the early disciples who proclaimed the Gospel of Christ to the world, sprang from the Jewish people.

As Holy Scripture testifies, Jerusalem did not recognise the time of her visitation,[4] nor did the Jews, in large number, accept the Gospel; indeed not a few opposed its spreading.[5]

---

[1] Cf. Galatians 3:7.
[2] Cf. Romans 11:17–24.
[3] Cf. Ephesians 2:14–16.
[4] Cf. Luke 19:44.
[5] Cf. Romans 11:28.

Nevertheless, God holds the Jews most dear for the sake of their Fathers; he does not repent of the gifts he makes or of the calls he issues—such is the witness of the Apostle.[1] In company with the prophets and the same Apostle, the Church awaits that day, known to God alone, on which all peoples will address the Lord with a single voice and "serve him with one accord" (Zephaniah 3 :9).[2]

Since then the spiritual patrimony common to Christians and Jews is so great, the Council wishes to foster and commend mutual understanding and esteem. This will be the fruit above all, of biblical and theological studies and of brotherly dialogues.

True, the Jewish authorities and those who followed their lead pressed for the death of Christ;[3] still, what happened in his passion cannot be charged against all the Jews, without distinction, then alive, nor against the Jews of today. Although the Church is the new People of God, the Jews should not be represented as rejected by God or accursed, as if this followed from the holy Scriptures. All should see to it, then, that in catechetical work and in the preaching of the word of God they teach nothing save what conforms to the truth of the Gospel and the Spirit of Christ.

Furthermore, in her rejection of every persecution against any man, the Church, mindful of the patrimony she shares with the Jews and led not by political reasons but by the Gospel's spiritual love, decries hatred, persecutions, manifestations of anti-semitism, directed against Jews at any time and by anyone.

[1] Cf. Romans 11:28–29; cf. Dogmatic Constitution on the Church, *Lumen Centium*, A.A.S., 57 (1965), p. 20.
[2] Cf. Isaiah 66:23; Psalm 65 (66):4; Romans 11:11–32.
[3] Cf. John 19:6.

Besides, Christ out of infinite love freely underwent his passion and death for the sins of all men in order that all may reach salvation. This the Church has always taught and teaches still; and it is therefore the duty of the Church to proclaim the cross of Christ as the sign of God's all-embracing love and as the fountain from which every grace flows.

5. *The Brotherhood of Man*

We cannot truly call upon the Father of all, if we refuse to treat in a brotherly way any class of men, created as all are in the image of God. Man's relation to God the Father and his relation to men his brothers are so linked together that scripture says "He who does not love does not know God" (1 John 4:8).

No foundation therefore remains for any theory or practice that leads to discrimination between man and man or people and people, so far as their human dignity and the rights flowing from it are concerned.

The Church reproves, as foreign to the mind of Christ, any discrimination against men or harassment of them because of their race, colour, condition in life, or religion. On the contrary, following the footsteps of the holy apostles Peter and Paul, the Council ardently implores the christian faithful to maintain good fellowship among the nations" (1 Peter 2:12), and, if possible, to live for their part in peace with all men,[1] so that they may truly be sons of the Father who is in heaven.[2]

[1] Cf. Romans 12:18.   [2] Cf. Matthew 5:45.

Appendix II

Addresses to the Council

a. Relatio *on the schema, November 1963*[1]

The schema "On the Jews" now up for examination was begun about two years ago, and in substance it was finished in May of last year (1962). This year, with the approval of the Council Co-ordinating Committee, it was placed in the schema "On Ecumenism".

The Secretariat to which the care of promoting Christian unity is given undertook treatment of the Jewish question not on its own initiative, but by the express command of the Supreme Pontiff, Pope John XXIII of happy memory. This was given verbally to the President of the Secretariat.

After this schema was prepared it was to have been discussed in the conferences of the Central Commission in June 1962. The discussion was omitted not because of the ideas or doctrine expressed in the schema, but only because of certain unhappy political conditions at that time.

The Decree is very brief, but the material treated in it is not easy. Let us enter immediately into the heart of it and say what we are talking about. Or rather, since it is so easy to understand it wrongly, before all else let us say what we are *not* talking about. There is no national or political question here. In particular, there is no question of recognition of the State of Israel by the Holy See. None of such questions are dealt with or even touched upon. The schema treats exclusively of a purely religious question.

[1] An English version of this has been published in *Council Speeches of Vatican II*, Sheed & Ward, London, 1964.

The Decree intends to recall in a solemn way those things which the Church of Christ, by hidden design of divine providence, receives through the hands of the chosen people of Israel. It receives first of all, in the words of St Paul in his Epistle to the Romans, "the oracles of God" (Romans 3:2); that is, the word of God in the Old Testament. Besides, to use the words of the same St Paul, to the Israelites "belong the son-ship, the glory, the covenants, the giving of the law, the worship, and the promises"; to them belong the patriarchs, and "of their race, accord-ing to the flesh, is Christ, who is over all things, God blessed forever" (Romans 9:5).

In other words, not only was the whole preparation of the work of the Redeemer and his Church done in the Old Testament, but also the execution of his work, the foundation of the Church and its propagation in the world were either in the chosen people of Israel or through members of this people whom God chose as instruments. The Church is in some sense the continuation of the chosen people of Israel, as is so well stated in the schema on the Church,[1] so that according to St Paul, Christians can be called "Israelites" not indeed "according to the flesh" but because in them are fulfilled the promises made to Abraham, the father of the people of Israel (cf Romans. 9:6–8). For in us Christians, members of the Church, the perfection of that kingdom of God for which God selected and designated the people of Israel is brought to fruition.

Indeed, it can justly be asked whether the language sometimes used by our preachers, especially in dealing with the passion of Christ, shows right appreciation of these facts, of the relations of the Church to the chosen people of Israel and of the gratitude due from us to this people.

There are those who object: Did not the princes of this people, with the people in agreement, condemn and crucify the innocent Christ, the Lord? Did they not "clamour": "His blood be on us and on our children" (Matthew 27:25)? Did not Christ himself speak most severely about Jews and their punishment?

I reply simply and briefly: It is true that Christ spoke severely, but

1 *Constitution on the Church*, Ch. II, n. 9.

only with the intention that the people might be converted and might "recognise the time of its visitation" (cf. Luke 19:42-8). But even as he is dying on the cross he prays: "Father forgive them, for they know not what they do" (Luke 23:24).

Wherefore, since the Lord declared, before the burial of Lazarus, speaking to the Father: "I know that thou always hearest me" (John 11:42), it is wrong to say that his prayer to the Father was not heard and that God has not only not forgiven the fault of his chosen people but that he has rejected them.

God himself, through St Paul, assures us that he "in no way" has rejected his chosen and beloved people. For the apostle writes to the Romans: "I ask then: has God rejected his people? By no means . . . God has not rejected his people whom he foreknew" (Romans 11:1f). And a little later he gives the reason: "For the gifts and the call of God are irrevocable" (Romans 11:29), that is, God does not revoke a choice once made, nor does he reject the people of Israel. Going still further, St Paul affirms that at some time "all Israel" will be saved, both those who are of "Israel according to the flesh" as well as those who are of Israel according to the promise only. For the apostle states: "Lest you be wise in your own conceits, I want you to understand, brethren, a hardening has come upon part of Israel, until the full number of the Gentiles come in, and so all Israel will be saved . . . Just as you (the Romans insofar as they belonged to the non-Jewish people) were once disobedient to God but now have received mercy because of their disobedience, so they have now been disobedient in order that by the mercy shown to you they *also may receive mercy* (Romans 11:25ff. and 30ff.).

Hence St Paul, though he had suffered so much from some Jews, was yet able to say, expressing something of the burning charity of God: "I could wish that I myself were accursed and cut off from Christ for the sake of my brethren, my kinsmen by race" (Romans 9:3).

Therefore, the aim of this very brief decree is to call to the attention of Christ's faithful these truths concerning the Jews which are affirmed by the apostle and contained in the deposit of faith, and to do this so clearly that in dealing with the children of that people the faithful will act in no other way than did Christ the Lord and his apostles Peter and

Paul. St Peter, in preaching to the Jewish people on the crucifixion of the Lord, said, "I know that you acted through ignorance, as did also your rulers ..." (Acts 3:17). Thus he excuses even the rulers themselves. Likewise St Paul (Acts 13:27).

The point, therefore, is not in any way to call into doubt—as is sometimes falsely asserted—the facts which are narrated in the Gospels about Christ's consciousness of his dignity and divine nature, or about the manner in which the innocent Lord was unjustly condemned. Rather that, with these things kept fully in mind, it is still possible and necessary to imitate the gentle charity of Christ the Lord and his apostles, with which they found an excuse for their persecutors.

But why is it so necessary precisely today to recall these things? The reason is this. Some decades ago anti-Semitism, as it is called, was prevalent in various regions and in a particularly violent and criminal form, especially in Germany under the rule of National Socialism, which through hatred for the Jews committed frightful crimes, extirpating several million of Jewish people—we need not at the moment seek the exact number. Moreover, accompanying and assisting this whole activity was a most powerful and effective "propaganda" as it is called, against the Jews. Now, it would have been almost impossible that some of the claims of that propaganda did not have an unfortunate effect even on faithful Catholics, the more so since the arguments advanced by that propaganda often enough bore an appearance of truth, especially when they were drawn from the New Testament and from the history of the Church. Thus, since the Church in this Council is striving to renew itself by "seeking again the features of its most fervent youth" as John XXIII of venerable memory said (cf. Discourse of 14 November, 1960, AAS, 52 (1960), p. 960), it seems imperative to take up this question.

Not that anti-semitism, especially that of National Socialism, drew its inspiration from Christian doctrine, a quite false allegation. Rather, it is a question of rooting out from the minds of Catholics any ideas which perhaps remain fixed there through the influence of that propaganda. If Christ the Lord and the apostles who personally experienced the grievous effects of the crucifixion maintained an ardent charity towards their very persecutors, how much more must we be motivated by the same charity?

For the Jews of our time can hardly be accused of the crimes committed against Christ, so far removed are they from those deeds. Actually, even in the time of Christ, the majority of the chosen people did not co-operate with the leaders of the people in condemning Christ. Does not the Gospel say that an actual member of the Sanhedrim, namely Joseph of Arimathea, did not "consent to their purpose and deed" (Luke 23:51)? Again, those among them who cried out to Pilate "Crucify him" formed a very small part of the chosen people. Were not the leaders of the Jews unwilling to kill the Lord "during the feast, lest there be tumult among the people" (Matthew 26:5)?

If therefore not even all the Jews in Palestine or in Jerusalem could be accused, how much less the Jews dispersed throughout the Roman Empire? And how much less again those who today, after nineteen centuries, live scattered throughout the whole world?

But let us set aside these considerations. Let the example of ardent charity given by the Lord and the apostles be sufficient for us. To this example the Church must conform as perfectly as possible in its teaching about the passion and death of the Lord. In saying this we do not mean to state or to hint that anti-semitism usually or principally arises from a religious source, namely from what the Gospels recount concerning the passion and death of the Lord. We are all well aware that anti-semitism also has causes of a political, national, psychological, social and economic nature. But we affirm that the Church most certainly must imitate Christ's example of gentle charity towards the people through whom it received so many and such great benefits from God.

If and when, therefore, some or many Jews do anything to justify the accusations made against them, Christians will be mindful of the example of St Paul. When violently attacked by a number of the Jews, St Paul did indeed publicly denounce his persecutors, since they interfered either with his freedom to announce the word of the Lord, or with the freedom of men to believe the Gospel (cf. 1 Thessalonians 2:15f). At the same time, however, he testified that he loved them so ardently that he would wish to be "accursed and cut off from Christ" for them. In such fashion, therefore, the children of the Church should also make vigorous use of the peaceful weapons of truth, charity and patience, which weapons are surely most effective.

Lastly: since we are here treating a merely religious question, there is obviously no danger that the Council will get entangled in those difficult questions regarding the relations between the Arab nations and the State of Israel, or regarding so-called Zionism.

In December of last year I set out in writing for the Supreme Pontiff, Pope John XXIII of happy memory, a discussion of this question "Regarding the Jews". After a few days the Holy Father indicated to me his full approval.

The Supreme Pontiff himself did indeed write in this sense scarcely five months before his holy death. Certainly, I am not saying that the question which we are treating was settled by these words of his; for he wanted the Council to be free, just as his successor also unquestionably wishes it. I think, however, that these words of his are dear to all the most eminent and most excellent Fathers, and that at the same time they throw light on the way in which we must follow Christ.

However, for our purpose, of much more importance, in fact simply decisive, is the example of burning charity of the Lord himself on the cross, praying, "Father, forgive them for they know not what they do." This is the example to be imitated by the Church, the Bride of Christ. This is the road to be followed by her. This is what the schema proposed by us intends to foster and promote.

b. Relatio *on the schema, 25 October 1964*

Venerable Fathers,

1. My commendation of the Schema of a Declaration on Jews and Non-Christians cannot but begin with the fact that this Declaration is one in which public opinion has shown the greatest interest. There is scarcely any other schema about which so much has been written in the press of the world and in newspapers of wide circulation and influence. Whatever may be thought of this interest and of the value to be attached to it, the mere fact of its existence shows that on this subject the eyes of the world are upon the Church, and that on the approval or disapproval of this Declaration will largely hinge a favourable or unfavourable judgement of the whole Council.

This is not, of course, the sole or even the main reason why this Declaration is necessary. The Declaration is primarily needed in order that the Church may be faithful in following the example of Christ and his disciples in love for the Jews. Nevertheless, considerations largely external ought not to be overlooked. They show the impossibility of following the advice of some of the Fathers and removing the subject from the programme altogether. Our Secretariat has examined their reasons with close attention and has used all diligence to ensure that the text should be carefully revised to meet the wishes of the Council Fathers as hitherto expressed. Moreover, the Co-ordinating Commission of the Council knows that it has had to spend a great deal of time on this short document.

2. The revision was made like this. The short introduction at the beginning of the previous text has been elaborated and a second part has been added to the Declaration—both at the express wishes of the Fathers in the second Session in the "Aula". As a result, the schema now has two sections, nearly equal in length, one on the Jews, the other on non-Christians.

3. As to the section on the Jews, the text is now better constructed and achieves a clearer sequence of ideas. Some new ideas have been introduced, especially two quotations from the Epistle to the Romans on the prerogatives of the chosen people (9:4), and on Christian hope of the ultimate union of the Jews with the chosen people of the New Testament, that is the Church (Romans 11:25).

4. The central issue which caused the more important changes was the question of "deicide". We all know how widely this question was discussed in the press—without the slightest intervention of co-operation by the Secretariat. Consequently, I must now point out the major issues. The question is if and how the condemnation and death of Christ the Lord is to be laid to the charge of the Jews *as such*. Now many modern Jews claim that the principal reason for anti-semitism stems from the conviction of general Jewish guilt, and that this conviction is the source of the flood of evils and persecutions which the Jews have suffered through the centuries. This cannot be sustained. In my address given in this "Aula" a year ago on this schema, I clearly stated: "We are all well aware that there are many reasons for anti-semitism which are not

religious at all but are political, national, psychological, social and economic." And yet it is still true that not a few instances can be found in the history of different peoples where conviction of general Jewish guilt led Christians to consider and designate the Jews with whom they lived as members of a race rejected and cursed by God for "deicide" and so to despise or even persecute them. It is for this reason that the Jews today are most anxious that the Council should show itself opposed to this conviction of general Jewish guilt and should publicly and solemnly declare that our Lord's death is in no way to be laid to the charge of the Jewish people *as such*. We must now decide whether such a declaration by the Council is possible and if so, how should it be made, what should be its tenor?

I need scarcely say that there is not and cannot be any question of denying or attenuating anything affirmed in the Gospels. The issue must be carefully defined and it is this: The leaders of the Jerusalem Sanhedrim, although not democratically elected, yet, according to the ordinary understanding of those days, accepted by the scriptures, were regarded and must be regarded as the embodiment of legitimate authority among the people. Here lie the gravity and the tragedy of their action—the exercise of their authority in the condemnation and death of Christ. Yet how grievous was their guilt? Did those "rulers" of the people in Jerusalem fully understand the divinity of Christ and so become formally guilty of deicide? Our Lord on the cross said in his prayer to the Father: "Father, forgive them: for they know not what they do" (Luke 23:34). If this reason for forgiveness is no mere empty formula—God forbid—it surely shows that the Jews were far from full understanding of the crime they were committing. St Peter also, addressing the Jewish people on the crucifixion of Christ, repeated: "And now, brethren, I know that you acted in ignorance, as did also your rulers" (Acts 3:17). So St Peter finds an excuse even for the very rulers! So likewise does St Paul (Acts 13:27). Furthermore, whatever may have been the knowledge possessed by the leaders in Jerusalem, the case of the people is quite different: *can the whole Jewish people of that time, generally and without distinction, be held answerable for the proceedings of their leaders in Jerusalem,* which led to the death of Christ? Statistics show that in the apostolic age the Jews dispersed throughout the Roman

Empire numbered about 4,500,000: are all of them to be accused of the deeds done by the Sanhedrists on that first sad Good Friday? And even granting—which we do not grant—that the people of that time were as a whole responsible, by what right can their descendants today be held in any sense as guilty? Can any other case be found anywhere in which we blame a nation for the actions of its ancestors over 1900 years ago?

5. Our Secretariat was at pains to take account of the conditions of these different classes of people, so that the schema might, on the one hand, affirm according to the Gospel narratives the guilt of those who decided upon the crucifixion of Christ, and on the other, might not ascribe any guilt to the Jewish people as a whole, much less to the Jews of today. There is no need here to appeal to the fact that Christ died for all men. For this is no way means that guilt for the death of the Lord *in the historical order* (which alone is in question here) is to be transferred to all men, or that they were *in the historical order* the efficient cause of his death. On the other hand the Jews as such, whether then or now, should not be charged with a crime in which they had no part. I ask you therefore to bear this in mind when you make your decision about this section of the proposed Declaration.

Because of the difficulty of the subject, it is understandable that many different formulas were tried, one after the other, in the effort, also, to satisfy the wishes and the criticisms of the Fathers. The frequent consultations that ensued became known, as many of you are aware, to the general public (how, no one knows). In consequence, both Council Fathers and others, including non-Catholics and non-Christians petitioned that the question of "deicide" should receive some treatment. It would be tiresome to describe all the deliberations in detail. Suffice it to have indicated how we arrived at the text you have before you. One thing more may be added: these deliberations took a long time. Consequently we were unable to submit this part of the Declaration for examination by the members of the Secretariat. Since the Secretariat had dealt with all its other business at its March sitting, it was decided not to recall the members to Rome to discuss this one section. All that now remains, Venerable Fathers, is to examine and discuss this schema. As you see, it is a matter of high importance and likewise of great difficulty.

Our Secretariat will gratefully receive any suggestions you may make about this part of the Declaration, so that the affair may be settled in the best possible way, in accordance with the wishes of the Council.

6. Something remains to be said about the second part of the Declaration which deals with our relation to non-Christian religions. As I said last year when the general schema on Ecumenism was being discussed, many desired a fuller treatment of our relationships with non-Christians, and some Fathers asked also for a special mention of the Moslems. All now appreciate the importance of this subject, especially since representatives of various non-Christian religions everywhere seek some contacts with the Catholic Church, and since all religions today are surrounded by an increasing practical irreligion or a militant theoretic atheism. When our Secretariat first touched on this subject, there was no other Commission or Secretariat that could deal with it, the Secretariat for non-Christian religions not being set up until May of this year. The only solution, then, was for us to undertake this task ourselves. And so, with the help of some of the Council experts we set about working out a schema. This was carefully examined and the Coordinating Commission of the Council decided on 18 April last that three ideas should be basic: (1) God is the Father of all men, and they are his sons. (2) All men therefore are brothers. (3) Consequently all types of discrimination must be condemned, together with all use of force and persecution for national or racial reasons. The Secretariat set about acting on this decision as best it could.

In the actual working out of the schema, explicit mention was made, as many Fathers desired, of the Moslems. May I say that the section of the text which deals with them won approval from experts of great experience, namely, the Institute of Oriental Studies conducted by the Dominicans at Cairo, and the Fathers of the African Mission (the White Fathers) working at the Pontifical Institute for Oriental Studies in Tunisia.

Although all the other matters before the Secretariat were finished by the end of March, we could not submit this part to the members. This will now be possible, Venerable Fathers, after you have expressed your views on this schema.

7. Before I finish, a word may be added on the relation of this schema to the schema on Ecumenism. As you will recall from last year's discussions, many Fathers did not want to include this matter in the ecumenical schema. This is understandable, since "Ecumenism" strictly means activity for union among *Christians*. And yet, the close association between the Church, the chosen people of the New Testament, with the chosen people of the Old Testament is common to all Christians, and thus there is an intimate connection between the ecumenical movement and the matters discussed in this Declaration. Even so, the bonds between Christians are closer than those between Christians and Jews. Hence matters dealing with our relationships with the Jews have been omitted from the schema on Ecumenism, in the sense that they are not a chapter in the Decree itself, but instead form a separate Declaration added at the end of the Decree. This may perhaps meet all wishes, especially as the place where the Declaration is to appear is of minor importance.

May I conclude with a few words on the nature and importance of the questions to be dealt with in this proposed Declaration? They are matters of the greatest importance for the Church and for the modern world. As regards the Church's relations with non-Christians, the importance is evident from the fact that this is the first time in the history of the Church that the subject has been treated by any Council. Further, the Holy See has set up a special organisation to encourage contacts with non-Christian religions. The importance is also abundantly clear in the Encyclical of Pope Paul VI *Ecclesiam Suam* (6 August 1964) in which he outlined the tasks before the Church and spoke of our dialogue with non-Christians. We should also remember that we are dealing here with the relationships of Catholics to hundreds of millions of men, with the charity we owe them, and the brotherly help and co-operation.

As regards the Jewish people, it must again and again be made clear that the *question is in no sense political*, but is purely religious. We are not talking about Zionism or the political State of Israel, but about the followers of the mosaic religion, wherever in the world they may dwell. Nor is it our concern to honour and praise the Jewish people, or to exalt it above other nations, or to attribute special privileges to it. Some thought the schema defective in that it made no mention of the severe language used by our Lord both to the Jews and about them, nor any mention of the divine benefits of which their unbelief deprived them. Some therefore would claim that the schema does not give a fair picture of the real state of the Jews. If such is the opinion of the majority of the Fathers, we shall obviously have to examine the matter afresh. It may, however, be permitted me to issue an immediate warning that the purpose of the Declaration is in no sense to give a complete and detailed account of the state of the Jewish people. In that case, how much would have to be said, and what a mass of evidence would have to be provided! It is true that the Lord Jesus himself spoke both to them and about them with great severity as is recorded in St Matthew's Gospel; but this in every case he did out of charity towards them, so that they might be warned of threatening dangers, "might know the time of their visitation" (Luke 19:44), accept the graces he offered them and so be saved. And St Paul writes as follows to the Thessalonians about the Jews, "who killed both the Lord Jesus and the prophets, and drove us out, and displease God and oppose all men, by hindering us from speaking to the Gentiles that they may be saved, so as always to fill up the measure of their sins. But God's wrath has come upon them at last" (1 Thessalonians 2:15ff). Yet the same apostle says elsewhere: "I am speaking the truth in Christ . . . that I have great sorrow and unceasing anguish in my heart. For I could wish that I myself were accursed and cut off from Christ for my brethren . . ." (Romans 9:1–3). Here then is the purpose and scope of this Declaration, that the Church should imitate Christ and the apostles in their charity, and by this imitation itself find a renewal, recalling how God worked out our salvation, and how many benefits he has bestowed upon us through this people. Even as regards the condemnation and death of Christ, brought about at Jerusalem by the Jewish "rulers", we must imitate the charity of Christ on the cross, praying to the Father for them, and excusing his persecutors with the words "they know not what they do"; and imitate the charity of the prince of the apostles and of the apostle of the Gentiles. If the Lord while he actually suffered acted so towards his persecutors, how much more ought we to foster charity towards the Jews of today, who are entirely guiltless of that deed. While the Church in the Council is busy with self-renewal and, as Pope John XXIII of blessed memory expressed it, is eager to restore its youthful fervour, attention should be given to this matter also, so that in this too the Church may be renewed. Such renewal is so important that it is worth while to expose ourselves to the danger of some people abusing this Declaration for political ends Our duties are to truth and justice. Our duty is to be grateful to God: our duty is to imitate faithfully and as closely as possible Christ our Lord and his apostles Peter and Paul. In so doing the Church and this Council can never allow any political influence or motive to find a place.

c. Account of the Declaration, 20 November 1954[1]

Venerable Fathers,

This Declaration might well be compared to the biblical grain of mustard seed. Originally it was my intention to make a short and simple statement on the relation between the Church and the Jewish people But in the course of time, and particularly in the course of the discussions in this Assembly, this seed, thanks to you, has almost grown into a tree, in which all the birds of the air are nesting. In a sense all the non-Christian religions find a place in it just as the present Pope included all non-Christians in his Encyclical Letter *Ecclesiam Suam*: "those who follow the religion of the Old Testament, Moslems and those who belong to the religions of Africa and Asia." It was not easy to cover all these in the space of a few pages. In the first place, I would like to express my special gratitude to all those who have contributed, verbally or in writing, to the drawing up of this Declaration. Our Secretariat has taken pains to consider all suggestions honestly and sincerely in order to produce a document which would be, as far as possible, worthy of the discussion which led to it, and worthy of the Council. It will be for you to judge whether and to want extent it has succeeded.

I think a few remarks may assist you here. I will not deal with the many points of detail which you have read in the *Relatio* which the Secretariat has drawn up most carefully. I wish to touch only on the

[1] The account of the document given to the Council by Cardinal Bea, 20 November 1964.

most important and general questions which might help you to form a fair and balanced view of the Declaration.

First, the Presidents of the Council, the Co-ordinating Commission and the Moderators think that the Declaration should be made part of the Constitution on the Church as the title of the present Declaration suggests, speaking as it does of the relation of the *Church* to non-Christian religions. In order not to interrupt the flow of the argument of the Constitution, and so delay an early vote and promulgation, it now seems best to attach this new Declaration at the end of the Constitution on the Church as an Appendix. To attach it to the Constitution has the further advantage that its purely religious character would be emphasised, and any political interpretation would be thereby excluded.

At the same time, the weight and impact of the Declaration would be all the greater if it is added to a dogmatic Constitution, even though the aim of the Declaration is pastoral rather than dogmatic.

Also noteworthy is the increased size of the Declaration. Acting on several suggestions made her in the "Aula" during the past year, the Secretariat, with the approval of higher authority, decided to include within its scope the whole range of relations between the Church and non-Christian religions. As a result the present document, which covers the whole of this wide field was born. I will return briefly to this point later.

However carefully the Secretariat set itself to consider all the suggestions and requests it was clearly impossible to satisfy everyone. The Secretariat has indeed done its very best to do so as far as it could. Since it was a question of recognizing the salvific will of God and his benefits and also of condemning absolutely hatred and injustices so as to avoid hem in the future, the Church and the Council clearly had to be faithful to its charge, and could not keep silent. In this, the Secretariat has kept clearly in mind the advice of the apostle of the Gentiles to give offence to nobody (2 Corinthians 6:3), while not forgetting his other warning to remain at peace with all men *so far as it depends on you* (Romans 12:18) which, obviously, is not always possible. So in our case it was impossible to draw up a Declaration which would not, in any passage, be open to misinterpretation by one side and at the same time satisfy the other side. Besides, it must be borne in mind that it is more important to have such a Solemn Declaration by the Council than to satisfy everyone, even if that were possible.

In judging how necessary is this Declaration, we must consider that it is very important that the Church (and indeed the Christian world and world public opinion too) should, through this Declaration, be led to notice and ponder the problems here set out. In this way Christians and all mankind will be enabled to understand this Declaration more fully, and put it into practice. For the Declaration ought to lead to effective action. Its principles and spirit should inspire the lives of all Christians and all men, so that the dialogue explained by the Pope in the encyclical *Ecclesiam Suam* may be begun. It is here, in the fruits which this Declaration should and will have after the Council, that its main importance lies.

I may be permitted to underline in particular the importance of this Declaration in so far as it deals with non-Christian religions. No Council in the history of the Church, unless I am mistaken, has ever set out so solemnly the principles concerning them. This consideration must be given full weight. We are dealing with more than a thousand million men who have never heard of, or never recognised Christ and his redemptive work. Of course they can be saved if they obey the dictates of conscience. Nevertheless, on the Church lies the grave duty of initiating dialogue with them by every means she can find which will help her to do so. As the Declaration points out, this can be done by our acknowledgement of the spiritual and moral values which are present in each religion, and by our sincere respect for those who belong to them. After all, they are, as the well known Letter of the Holy Office to the Archbishop of Boston pointed out, united to Christ and his Mystical Body by an implicit faith provided they follow the dictates of an upright conscience (Dz-Sch. No. 3872), until such time as they fully recognise and share the riches of Christ. There is no doubt that by her efforts in this direction the Church may give them effective help towards that explicit and full participation.

Conclusions. Just now, when Christ's vicar on earth is about to travel to visit that great people who, as he said, represent the innumerable races and peoples of Asia, it would have been most appropriate if, by the grace of God, this Declaration could have been definitively promulgated. This is at present unfortunately impossible. But the preparation of this Declaration is a token given by the Church to these peoples who are separated from Christ. May God, through the intercession of the Blessed Virgin Mary and all the Saints who are patrons of the Council, grant that this Declaration may as soon as possible meet the hopes of many, both in and outside the Council.

d. Prior to the voting on the amendments to the Declaration, 14 October 1965[1]

Venerable Fathers,

Please allow me to make a few observations before the vote is taken on the amendments proposed to the Declaration on the *Relation of the Church to Non-Christian Religions.* The Secretariat for Fostering Christian Unity has gratefully considered all the proposed amendments (*modi*). It has diligently and sincerely examined them but, as almost always happens, it has judged that some should be accepted, others not. No other criterion has been followed in this examination than that the schema should as far as possible become clearer and more accurate so that *the substance of the text* which you approved last year by a large majority *may be faithfully retained.*

In the first three chapters it seems that the intention of the Declaration is now expressed more clearly. It does not propose to offer a complete account of religions nor of the divergences that exist among themselves and from the Catholic religion. Rather, the Council intends through this Declaration to point out the bond between men and religions as the foundation of dialogue and co-operation. Thus, the stress is placed on those things which *unite* men and lead to mutual fellowship. There is need, of course, of prudence, but also of confidence and love. The *modi* and observations which you proposed have greatly helped us, so that now this Declaration, by which the Catholic Church for the first time proposes fraternal dialogue with the great non-Christian religions, better fulfils its purpose.

Chapter Four has required the most attention, both because of the

1 Given to the Council by Cardinal Bea, 14 October 1965.

seriousness of the question there treated and because of the many and diverse proposed modifications. The method used by the Secretariat was this: besides an accurate examination of the proposed *modi* in prolonged discussions, we judged that many journeys should be made to contact members of both the Catholic and non-Catholic hierarchies of those various regions in which greater difficulties have arisen during the past year because of this schema. All efforts have aimed: (1) to give no occasion, so far as possible, for less exact interpretations of Catholic doctrine in the proposed schema, (2) to assure the clear expression of the exclusively *religious* nature of the schema, so as to close off any opening to political interpretation.

(1) Concerning the last point, the Secretariat judged that in the condemnation of persecution against the Jews the motive of this condemnation be clearly expressed by inserting: "the Church, moved not by political reasons but by the Gospel's spiritual love, decries", and adds the reprobation of *any kind* of persecution against anyone. Thus the text now reads: "Moreover, the Church, which rejects every persecution against any man, mindful of the common patrimony with the Jews and moved not by political reasons but by the Gospel's spiritual love, decries hatred, persecution, displays of anti-semitism, directed against Jews at any time and by anyone." It is hoped that at least in this way, aside from repeated statements, every political interpretation of the decree, given by anyone whatever will be definitely excluded or at least the falsity of such an interpretation be clearly shown.

(2) As for *theological clarity* allow me explicitly to recall one point, the most difficult point of the schema, which concerns the question of the responsibility of the Jews for what happened in the passion of the Lord. To explain this clearly, I will first read the new text proposed by the Secretariat:

"Although the Jewish authorities and those who followed their lead pressed for the death of Christ (cf. John 19:6), nevertheless what happened in his passion cannot be attributed to all Jews, without distinction, then alive, nor to the Jews of today. Although the Church is the new people of God, the Jews should not be presented as rejected by God or accursed, as if this follows from the Holy Scriptures."

From this text it appears clear that:

1. The schema completely preserves and expounds the truth of the Gospel.

2. At the same time it excludes unjust affirmations and accusations made against all Jews, without distinction, then living and against the Jews of today: namely, that all of them are guilty of the condemnation of the Lord and therefore are rejected by God and accursed.

3. The Council exhorts everyone when dealing with this subject, especially in catechism instruction and preaching, to say only what accords with the truth of the Gospel and with the spirit of Christ.

By a comparison of this text with that approved by you last year it is clear that the Secretariat proposes that the expression "guilty of deicide" (*deicidii rei*) be eliminated from the text. Why? It is known that difficulties and controversies—for example, that the schema might seem to contradict the Gospel—have *in fact* arisen, especially because of the use of this word. On the other hand, it is obvious to anyone who reads the text, just now read and explained, that the *substance* of what we wished in the earlier text to express by this word is found exactly and completely expressed in the new text. I well know that some give great psychological, as the current term has it, importance to this word. Nevertheless, I say: if this word is misunderstood in so many regions, and if the same idea can be expressed by other more apt words, then does not pastoral prudence and Christian charity forbid us to use this word, does it not require that we explain the matter in other words? I say that this is required by the same "religious, evangelical love" which impelled John XXIII to order that this Declaration be prepared and which last year inspired you to approve it. Our Secretariat judged this emendation to be of great importance, in order that the Declaration itself be everywhere rightly understood and accepted, in spite of the various difficulties. Thus, I strongly urge you to consider this emendation in the light of pastoral prudence and evangelical charity.

Our Declaration looks to co-operation in that same mission to which the Supreme Pontiff dedicates himself in his encyclical letters, in his allocutions and in his acts. It is the mission, of which it is written: "Blessed are the peace-makters, for they shall be called sons of God"

(Matthew 5:9). It is the misson to which the entire work of the Prince of Peace was directed, he who through the cross had made, in himself, Jews and Gentiles into one new man, making peace, thus made our peace (cf. Ephesians 2:14–16). Following faithfully the work of its Head and spouse, the Church today is also considering more attentively how it can foster and further unity and concord among men and nations. May God grant that, through the intercession of the Blessed Virgin and of all the holy patrons of the Council, this Declaration by your work and prayer be an efficacious instrument in carrying out this mission.